EXCERPTS FROM

THE PAUL SOLOMON TAPES

ORIGINAL WRITING

Originally Published in 1974 by
Fellowship of the Inner Light, Virginia Beach, VA, USA

Republished in Ireland in 2013 by
ORIGINAL WRITING LTD, Spade Enterprise Center,
North King Street, Smithfield, Dublin 7, Republic of Ireland

ISBN-13: 978-1490982397
ISBN-10: 1490982396

To order additional copies, please contact:
The Paul Solomon Foundation Ltd.
www.paulsolomon.com
info@paulsolomon.com

Also available from: Amazon
www.amazon.com

Disclaimer About Medical Information:
The medical information and reference materials contained in this book are intended
solely for the general information of the reader.

It is not to be used for treatment purposes, but rather for discussion with the patient's
own physician. The information presented here is not intended to diagnose health
problems or to take the place of professional medical care. The information contained
herein is neither intended to dictate what constitutes reasonable, appropriate or best
care for any given health issue, nor is it intended to be used as a substitute for the
independent judgment of a physician for any given health issue.

This book is dedicated to
Our Father...
may He use it to awaken His sleeping Sons
And Daughters.

Preface

We became tremendously excited upon listening to the first tape of extracts from Paul Solomon's psychic readings. This material contains a wealth of inspirational spiritual guidance and psychic information on a fascinating variety of topics. We experienced a feeling of extreme humility and a sense of awe when Rev. Solomon and the Fellowship of the Inner Light, the organization of which he is founder, accepted our offer to publish his material.

Does the name of Solomon create an image in your mind of the Biblical King Solomon, noted for his wisdom? Apparently, this is intended. For the name of Paul Solomon is actually a pseudonym, suggested in an early reading for symbolic purposes. Rev. Solomon's training as an ordained minister with a Master's in Religious Education, together with his interest in metaphysical studies, provide a rich and interesting background for the spiritually oriented information for which he is a channel.

Paul Solomon's meeting with the Heritage Store was no accident. The Heritage Store has been involved since 1969 with making the natural formulas and remedies for physical ailments suggested in Edgar Cayce's psychic readings available to the public. More recently, we have become interested in the valuable information coming through other psychics as well and have pursued our own investigations in this field.

The reader will find that in tone and subject matter, Paul Solomon's readings often correspond closely to those of other well-known psychics, but in many cases shed light on new and unexplored areas. The emphasis of the Solomon readings on self-reliance and attunement to the spirit within is consistent and often inspirational. The selection of readings in this book consists of extracts derived from readings for individuals. And topics of discussion are varied enough that everyone will find something of interest.

In order to make the content of the readings more easily understandable, they have been edited slightly by inserting articles and pronouns where desirable. Other inserted words and phrases have been bracketed. On rare occasions, words or meanings were unintelligible. In these cases, ellipses (. . .) were used.

The reader will find a wide variety of topics discussed in each chapter and sometimes within each reading. Rather than separating all of the readings into specific chapter headings, we found it in some cases more valuable to leave a major portion, or even an entire reading, intact. Thus selections within each chapter will sometimes be found to overlap with other chapters in subject matter.

On a larger scale, we feel that the "wisdom of Solomon" will eventually prove to be a major contribution to metaphysical literature, and thus add to the growing body of spiritual and metaphysical knowledge that is our heritage. Future publications should continue to support us in this view.

Tom Johnson

Introduction

On February 15, 1972, a hypnotized man speaking in sleepy, mumbling, incoherent tones suddenly jerked violently as if some unseen force had struck him in the solar plexus. The anxiety of the young amateur hypnotist, now shaken and startled by this unexpected reaction, was hardly relieved by the powerful, stern voice which immediately began to speak through the now rigid body of the hypnotized man: "You have not attained sufficient growth or spiritual awareness to understand contact with these records! That which you perform is a foolish experiment, for you attempt to harness powers you do not understand and to contact sources, records or intelligence you are not familiar with. And how will you try the spirits, should you attain that you seek? Would you recognize Him whom you do not know, have not been familiar with?"

The young hypnotist recovered sufficiently to attempt asking questions here, hoping to gain some clue to the nature or source of the voice that spoke: "Are you a 'familiar spirit' or a spirit guide and can you give us your name?"

"Neither familiar spirit nor guide is needed for the reading of these records. It is rather in yourselves, in your own development that understanding will come and guidance – not from a lesser spirit, but from the Throne of Grace – that you may come before these records and read what you will for the instruction and development of those on your plane who would know more of the Divine. Then go, study with much prayer and meditation – develop the self and spiritual understanding that you may return, and, being familiar with these planes, you will be welcomed and may read and rejoice."

As suddenly as the voice had begun its unexpected discourse, it now ceased with a second sudden violent jerk of the body. Paul Solomon doubled up as if hit in the abdomen and now lapsed into an apparently normal deep sleep.

Trying hard to conceal and contain his excitement, Joel Spires III (not his real name) began the task of patiently counting his subject up and out of the hypnotic sleep. The simple waking exercise, which takes only a few moments, seemed endless in his excitement. And the necessary calm he must project seemed impossible as he tried to organize his thoughts and assess the importance of what had just taken place.

Finally it was done. Paul Solomon, dazed and confused was awake. But something was wrong. He clutched his stomach in pain and needed help to stand. Although the pain was short lived, he remained irritable for some time and certainly did not share the excitement of Joel for 'strange voices' speaking through his sleeping body. In fact, the only thing that impressed him about his first experience with being hypnotized was his only memory of what had actually taken place and that was the pain! He remembered only drifting off pleasantly and waking very suddenly to excruciating cramps in his abdomen. As far as repeating the experiment so that the voices could be recorded, he wanted no part of it.

Thus began the Paul Solomon Readings. It took some time and some persuasion to convince Paul Solomon that another attempt should be made. But with questions prepared and testing procedures agreed upon, including the presence of a very skeptical friend, the second reading was recorded. Nothing of historical significance was said in the second reading except for the voices pointing out that they were quite aware that the third party present was in trouble with the authorities and that they could and would be glad to instruct him in correcting the problem, but would do so only when he was ready to accept the instructions and when he really wanted to correct the situation. For the present, they would only heal his physical condition.

The physical condition, which had resulted from a drunken fight and had left him miserable, was indeed healed instantly! This began a new life for the young man, AWOL and troubled, a heavy drinker with certainly no interest in 'spiritual growth.' Only because of the pro-found wisdom of the instruction and the loving guidance of the "Paul Solomon Source" is Tony now happily married and following a successful career as a U. S. Army chaplain.

It was during this second reading that Paul Solomon learned that he could avoid the pain associated with leaving his body by understanding the cause of it. He also learned that he must follow a rigorous six-month program of mental, physical and spiritual discipline and development, to obtain efficient use of this gift for helping himself and others in the attempt to understand a purpose in life and to develop their full potential.

In more than 300 hours of these trance readings for individuals, Paul Solomon has received instruction and comments on virtually every phase of human existence. There are medical diagnoses and suggestions for treatment, which have been proved to be accurate and beneficial when used under medical supervision. There are prophecies, which have been borne out in fact. There is a wealth of wisdom and instruction in spiritual growth and enlightenment, and even a com-plete system for development of spiritual gifts or psychism, which is taught under the name, "Inner Light Consciousness."

The Fellowship of the Inner Light is a non-profit, open-membership organization with headquarters in Virginia Beach. The Fellowship offers several categories of membership, each with attractive benefits. And you are invited to inquire further.

EXCERPTS FROM THE PAUL SOLOMON TAPES is a selection of passages from the tape recordings of the Paul Solomon Readings. We have selected these particular quotes (difficult as it is to isolate the best) for their universal significance and appeal. Our task in selecting was made somewhat easier by the knowledge that other books are in preparation to cover such specific subjects as: "Paul Solomon on Healing," "The Wisdom of Solomon" (a collection of cases in which the Paul Solomon Readings proved accurate and important enough to affect the life of the seeker), "Paul Solomon on Sex," etc.

Many readers will want to explore further the concepts found in THE PAUL SOLOMON TAPES, as well as related background material. Both the Fellowship and the publishers have a list of related books that will shed more light on the subjects contained within this volume. We dedicate this book to the realization among men that God is indeed alive and well and that His prophets exist in this day.

James Allen Wharton,
now James Daniel Emmanuel
Associate Pastor
FELLOWSHIP OF THE INNER LIGHT
Virginia Beach, Virginia 23458

Contents

PREFACE   v

INTRODUCTION   vii

SPIRIT GUIDES   Pages 1- 10

Masters of unknown identity   Excerpt 1
Spirit guides versus Holy Spirit   2
Recognizing the true guide   3
The master within   4
Spiritual teachers in every experience   5

ATLANTIS & PREHISTORY   Pages 11–37

Creation and evolution   Excerpt 6
Astrology and the destiny of free will   7
Earth changes in ancient Lemuria   8
Atlantean crystals and flying machines   9
Geodesic force fields and pyramid power   10
Natural energies in food preparation and survival   11
An Atlantean immigrant in North America   12
Secrets of the Hall of Records   13

DIET & HEALTH   Pages 38 – 47
Concerning a vegetarian diet   Excerpt 14
The consciousness of food in ancient Lemuria   15
A diet for a dancer   16
Dietary practices in ancient Atlantis and today   17
The implications of fasting   18
Purification of the body through diet and discipline   19

HEALING   Pages 48 – 74

Tapping unlimited energies   Excerpt 20
The power of faith in healing   21
An experiment in group healing   22
Raising the vibrations of the body   23
Understanding the laws of healing   24
Healing of children through thought transference and massage 25
The healing ministry of comedy   26
Healing arts from the temple Beautiful   27
The healing harp   28
Tuning in to color fields   29
A study of plants and vibration   30

MUSIC AND ART   Pages 75 – 89

Advice to a talented musician: attuning
to the music of the spheres   Excerpt 31
The great potential of music in spiritual growth   32
Music as therapy for the mind and body   33
Art as a healing influence   34

REINCARNATION & KARMA   Pages 90 – 106

Miscellaneous questions concerning reincarnation   Excerpt 35
How to erase karmic debt   36
An incarnation with Jesus and a meeting
with the Lords of Karma   37
Witness to the crucifixion   38
Persecution of the early Christians   39
Evolution of the soul   40

SEX & RELATED TOPICS   Pages 107 – 126

A morality of sex   Excerpt 41
Sexual energy and spiritual growth   42
Sex and the single person   43

Sex and temptation   44
The beginning of sex   45
Soul attraction, conception and abortion   46
A new method of birth control   47
The effect of mental attitudes in conception and contraception   48
The astrological birth time of the soul   49

SOUL DEVELOPMENT   Pages 127 – 147

The earth as a spiritual symbol   Excerpt 50
Media: food for the mind   51
Dedication and inner direction   52
How to know God   53
Birth from the spiritual womb   54
The challenge of temptation   55
Dying daily to the world   56
The meaning of dreams   57
A guide to working with dreams   58
Dream symbology and visitations   59
Travel and learning experiences during sleep   60

SPIRITUAL GROWTH & TEACHINGS   Pages 148-171

The Bible and the inner voice   Excerpt 61
Mental obesity   62
The true church   63
Parable of Job   64
The nature of Hell   65
A message from the angel Halaliel   66
Master over mockery   67
The Kabala, the Christ and spiritual awareness   68
Drugs and the kundalini   69
Marijuana and meditation   70
Evolutionary keys to spiritual growth   71

WORLD PROPHECY   Pages 172 -187

Coming of the Aquarian Age Christ   Excerpt 72
Scientific marvels of tomorrow   73
Earth changes and the new race   74
Times of trial and testing   75
Atlantis rises again   76
Israel: the last battle   77
Women in power   78
Parable of the black God   79
The comet Kohoutek: sign in the sky   80
Christ and the Anti-Christ   81

A FINAL WORD   Pages 188 -189

A message for all   Excerpt 82

Spirit Guides

Conductor: Will I in this lifetime attain spiritual enlightenment, that is cosmic consciousness, or the level at which I am free of all karmic bondage?

And [considering] those questions as have been brought ... we would take great pleasure in attempting to bring to the surface and this heart that answer which has been evasive for this one, that has been so near the surface and yet unable to express in this lifetime. For we would find those questions as concern the development of the masters or the necessity for a master in this lifetime, and the manner in which one would deal with such spiritual teachers – whether in manifestation or on spiritual planes.

And we would have this one open the eyes that he might see that there have been used those upon this plane that have shown great beauty of intellect and those abilities to demonstrate the powers of God, whether in healing or in speaking words of truth, whether being channels for great teachings or writings, or those talented preachers or speakers – those who have conquered the laws of your universe and could demonstrate the power of God, and have been established as great spiritual teachers and leaders. And there have been given and have appeared those angels of light, those prophets of old, both in dreams and visions and walking even apparently manifest upon your earth, that they might teach this one or another who so needed instruction in spiritual growth. And there have been those other instruments as needed, whether that you know as Bible or scripture, or those other inspired writings that are given for purposes of understanding development. And we would find those on your plane seeking to develop within, seeking to understand the rules of the manners or methods by which spiritual growth may be attained and cosmic consciousness realized.

And there have been established those methods, those tools, that these would follow; and yet we would find that the very seeking, the very use of these tools, the following of these masters, these teachers, the recognition of these has in itself placed a block before the mental development, the spiritual development that would allow one so close to cross the threshold to cosmic consciousness. And why would we find it so? We would find in this way: That whether a man speak with the tongue of the gods, or speak as an angel, or appear as a minister of mercy or a prophet or a sage – whether one be a healer or worker of miracles – if one would call himself a master, a teacher, or a guide and would cause this one or that to be a student or to follow him in his teachings, his methods, would not the student then have his attention focused upon the master, the teacher, the method, the tool? And is this not then the subtle diversion from truth? For truth itself lies one step beyond the tool, the master, the teacher, even the spirit guide.

And know that there is not one on your plane or on inner planes who is a master that would call himself a master. For there is not one who is a servant of the Divine that would attract attention to himself and in so doing become a stumbling block or divert attention from that perfection that is you. And if thou wilt attain cosmic consciousness in this lifetime, it would not be through a teacher, either on your earth or on this plane; or through a tool whether it be scripture [or] whether it be a technique – for meditation, for discipline, for development of any kind.

Then, what would so bring cosmic consciousness? It would come only through awakening, through realizing that all that is needed and indeed all that there is lies within yourself and not in another heart. And anyone on your plane who would speak the words of God can only divert your attention from that voice that is the true teacher.

Now it has been realized in this heart that truth lies in meditation and in the quietness, in the stillness. And yet, have you not been given that that would play over and again in the mind and that voice that is a mechanical tool; that sound, that vibration that is a mechanical tool for producing an effect – would it not in itself divert attention from that central truth that would well up naturally, if this quietness were to become prime central stillness?

For it is here that you will find Him who is not only the expression of the Almighty, but is as well the expression of yourself. And as He is born and begins to live in this body, so will this body attain cosmic consciousness, for his identity is consciousness of God. There are no limits to that which this one could attain in this lifetime.

And in dealing with those questions as are brought, we would give in this manner that there would and should be the teaching of the meditation techniques, but as well [there] should be given the diversion from worshiping a technique or a master or a teacher or a method. Broaden your realization to know that that one who has failed in this lifetime and is found in the gutter – when he crosses your attention and teaches a lesson he is the master and was set there for a purpose. And as you would learn the lesson from seeing his failure, his fault, even his sin, has he not taught well the lesson that he was set there to teach?

You have met masters in this lifetime but never have you recognized one. There have been spirit guides, those who came to teach, but never have you realized them. And it is to their credit that it is so. For a master who would allow himself to be recognized as a master would have failed in his mission, and would by definition no longer be a master. Know whom you would serve. And know that as He is expressed in all men on your planet and all men on inner planes, so as well is He not expressed in anyone? So in that paradox you would find truth. For those about you who would be the expressions of the One whom you would serve, the One whom you would become, these about you only are statements of Him. He Himself dwells in your own heart. It is here that you will find Him.

And it is in recognizing Him that you will realize that that one you consider a teacher is by his very existence a limitation. And it will not be until you have gone beyond his identity, his limitation and even his wisdom, his teaching, that you would see that which he has failed to attain and express and understand is in your own heart.

And you will awaken with the realization that you have surpassed all the teachings, all the expressions of all who are the teachers on your planes, and yea, on all planes. And you would see even the angels in Heaven rejoice and gather about to worship even their teacher, their master. And in that moment you will realize that thou are He, and all that stood between your realization of who He was and is, is that which you know as ego, or personality, or self.

For as long as you value identity, personality, or self, you find that barrier between self and expression of the Divine. And that moment that identity is lost and thou shalt become Him – in that moment shall thou express cosmic consciousness and His presence on this earth plane. And in that moment shall the scales be lifted from your eyes and you shall observe the Second Coming of the Christ.

Now understand these teachings and attune self to Self. Release identity. Place your value on those things that are of value, lest true value be taken away.

3014 (2-3-73)

EXCERPT 2

Conductor: Do I have a spirit guide? If so how do I become better attuned to Him?

Now concern the self not so much with the spirit guide. Yet there are those that hover about and seek to be of assistance in the development. Yet, if you would know him there need be the much development or the guidance in such ways or some such programs as have been instructed from these records, from these planes. And others have developed such manners, such means for contacting same, yet [it is] not necessary that you understand the individuality or personality of a spiritual guide, for understand that these are only assistants to point beyond themselves to the Father.

Then seek the Father and not the guide, for these only are given as indicators, as markers along the way, and it is not the signpost that you would seek to be attracted to, but that to which the sign would point.

4030 (7-24-73)

EXCERPT 3

Conductor: Do I have a spirit guide? And if so, how do I communicate with him?

Now we find these answers have been given, but will be given briefly from this plane in this manner. That same One who set the example, who made possible redemption for those of this age, that same Spirit that was his guide, that same Spirit that He promised and left is available and is that Spirit with whom you should communicate within. There is no greater, there is no closer, there is no superior, there is no more personal spirit guide than this One. If others would seek to assist from inner planes, they should be taken only as servants, as messengers, never as guides or superior beings that would show to those on this plane the will of the Father. Is the Father incapable of direct communication? Would not that Holy Spirit of the Father Himself live within your own heart and how could another either incarnate or discarnate be closer and know His will in a closer way than even this one within her own heart?

Now attune to self and attune self to the will of the Father and claim the blessing, claim the presence of that Divine Spirit that lives within, for this is your spirit guide.

1007 (12-1-72)

EXCERPT 4

It should be taught as well that these ones who come asking about spirit guides would concern themselves not with spirit guides, but with Spirit. All that is needed from inner planes is given to every person on your plane, and when there is sought the development along spiritual planes there are sent teachers or influences. They are so often thought of in your time and mind as another entity that would come in and teach you this or that, as you know teachers on your plane. Realize that if a beautiful star in the heavens can influence the thought within your mind, and [has] brought a little beauty into your life – that this inanimate star itself was a teacher, it was a spirit guide. If there is a tree that impressed you with the beauty of its form, and in it you saw some of God revealed in nature, this tree was for you a spirit guide. It was used of Spirit as a teacher.

Seek not then that there would be an entity, a personality, someone who may be labeled spirit guide, spirit teacher. These things so often are discarnate spirits and these are not [of] the nature of those that would come to you from inner planes as spirit guides. If you would know the true guide, if you would know true spirit, realize that within you there is a spark of the Divine Creator that is capable of creating universes within itself. This spark of the Divine Creator is greater than any guide, than any teacher that would manifest on your plane or would come in dreams or otherwise. This spark of life, this spark of God, the spark of good, the spark of light itself is you. It is the You of you. It is the Identity of you. All that you may know of God is written on this tablet of your own heart. This is the Light. This Light came into the world, came into darkness and darkness knew it not. It is in your life and you know it not.

Recognize, realize this spark of God and see God Himself as your spirit guide. Seek to turn inward and to fan this spark into flame and follow these indications. Seek not from outside sources but from deep within those things that would be of God.

Realize that all influences that come into your life, and that indicate this direction or that – these are the spirit guides, these are the teachers. Realize that the masters who have gone on before when they send this indication or that to teach you in their way – that they seek not to draw attention to themselves, but away from themselves and to that spark of your Divine Self. Those spirit guides, those teachers, those masters who influence your life seek to turn you away from them, away from identifying, realizing, knowing them, and to turn you inward. This is the purpose of a spirit guide: to detract attention from himself, to point attention instead to the God force, to the life force that is within you.

Bypass then those people who are following spirit guides, [and] go beyond them, go deeper, go inside. Realize the Godhead attempting to manifest through you and to shine His light into the world. See yourself as a light bulb, see yourself as a container of that light that would shine forth from inside you out into the world. Seek to be a light in the midst of darkness. Seek to use your tiny flame as a candle in this world of darkness, and seek that everyone who comes in contact with you would be lifted a little closer to the God force.

As to the spiritual guide, there are those who would seek from inner planes to bring this one a little closer to God, that would teach this one the path and the means of developing towards the One that is God. It would be seen in this manner as has been given so often before, and as will continue to be given from this source: It should be realized that whether Rafael, Halaliel or one of the other archangels, or simply one of past incarnations who has passed on to inner planes or higher planes; whether it would be that who would come and speak to this one as a spirit guide or that [who would] simply teach this one – these would not become known by name or by address for the reason that He who would be seen as your guide, as all that He is in your life, as the light, as the one who would lead you closer to God would be the Christ and there will be no other between Him, there will be no other besides Him, there will be no other equal to Him. And if these names of guides or angels or those who would seek to teach the masters from the inner planes worthy of them [were revealed], would this not distract then from Him who was thy guide, Him whom is thy light, that great leader, the one who became the Christ, the one who showed the way?

Follow this example. Do this. Ask the Spirit Guide. Realize that there is none closer, [and that] it is not possible that one could become closer within the heart of the light. And if there would be one inclined from this plane as a teacher, as a master, as a guide, would not it be said, and would not this one want to realize that he is one with God, he is one with the Christ? Therefore, there need be no other affinity, no other name given and will not be given from these planes, from these sources. If there are names that come in the night, if there is a name whispered, a name realized that is repeated again and again in the head, then this one would be that spirit guide, and you would know this force to be one from the inner plane and one who seeks to help and teach and guide; and only in this manner would the name of the spirit guide be given. Do not accept those names that are given from outside sources as might be given through these that would speak, for these always will come from within. But never should these be confused with or put before Him who was the Christ, who ... is the Christ, He who would lift you to the Christ Consciousness. Seek these things in thine own relationship and thou wilt be made perfect in the law of God.

1015 (4-11-73)

EXCERPT 5

Conductor: Why haven't I been contacted from spiritual guides?

This we find as being misunderstood in this mind or in this manner of asking. Be aware that such teachers have been contacted and surround the self often, and such indications ... [that have] come often in the life are the teachings of the masters, the teachers, the spiritual guides. Now understand that ... which you are led into and away from. Though you hear not a voice, though you see not a presence, though you may not be aware of that which does the leading or causes these things to fall in place the way they do, [even] so the lessons are provided. It is a credit to that one which provides guidance from inner planes that you are not often aware of his presence and never aware of his identity. For in being aware of his presence or identity, would you not be distracted from that lesson he provides, placing then your attention upon him? But be aware that rather than knowing him and his presence in being identified with an individual personality, rather [learn] that which he would have you know, which he would teach ... provided always in perfect lessons.

Know that this is a master, a teacher of very high level and should be much respected, though his identity may never be known, and it will be to his credit that it should be so. Then seek not to know his identity or personality, but observe those lessons placed in this life, for much importance has been given to this one's growth and always those incidents will come – that which needs be reacted [to] will be provided. For such a one with [such] a background – these past lives that have been built – the bringing in, this one would not be neglected by those who seek to carry on His message on this plane, on this sphere. Be aware that you have been entrusted with an impor-tant one, and both have come from those periods of the Atlantean times when there was such a diametric opposition between those forces or those sons of God and the sons of Belial. And does not this opposition became even so important in this day that you have much to fight against and there is dichotomy set up upon this plane at this time? Such extremes have come, for these Atlanteans always have been a nation of extremes and have no middle ground.

We know that that which we would bring as influences into the life of the child and that which we would bring in the self, in the developments of these talents, have been brought – and the understanding. Be aware of the necessity to know the Christ force, for how fortunate you have been to be aware of that which He built – this particular Master. Know the importance of the Christ and that which He created, for this is that which separates the sons of God from the sons of that evil one in that time. For those Atlanteans who recognized God and served the Law of One in that time of Atlantis – so these same ones were exposed to the Christ when He walked upon this earth. And this is the reason that you have such an influx in this day, not only of those who lived in the times of that land but as well of those who walked with Him when He was on this earth and were aware of His presence and the changes that He made. These are the sons of the Law of One, not the sons of Belial, for very few of those are aware of that which He created and the necessity for meeting those karmic debts as were part of their life and that which they built in that time before they lost such power. But know that they come in this day with a memory of that power, yet without the knowledge of the Law of One.

So does not your job become greater even than in that day – those of you who are aware of what this Master produced and of the Christ power that is available in the world today? Then look not for a master or a spiritual guide, but for understanding of that which He brought. Understand the Christ and the Christ force; understand that it works from the beginning – even of those periods of Atlantis before the man Jesus walked the earth.

So was the Christ power, the law of One, available, and still even in this day. If you have awareness then of Him, seek Him as thy master, thy teacher. And be aware that that one which would teach from inner planes is one which would have thee understand and follow such teachings in this time, and know that you are surrounded by his presence and all that you need react to, all that you need learn are placed in thy path. Learn from each time that such things occur. Recognize that which is stimulated within the heart, within the conscience, within the knowledge, within the self. That which you recognize as truth, accept it as if it were gold and apply in the life.

Know the importance of being awakened to the Christ force. Never let it become small with thee. Know the importance of this lifetime, for these are the last days and there is much to be done with one with such great talent, there is much to be accomplished. Be about the Father's business in all that you do.

7025 (4-30-73)

Atlantis & Prehistory

Read in your Book: God created the lights, the earth, the firmament, and He looked upon the earth and His stars, and moon, and the sun, all these things, and saw that they were good. And as God smiled upon creation, He called the Sons of God together. And the Sons of God [were] all those entities that were part of His soul. As God moved, these soul entities broke off from His body and spread about ... as you might say, frolicking, enjoying the pleasures, the beauty of God's creation.

So the Sons of God would be the beginnings of you and me. They moved over the waters and through the light. There was singing and music, the singing, the laughter of the children of God. And God saw that it was good. And all these entities, as parts of their Creator, of the nature of the Creator, then were, in themselves, creators, through the power of God. We would see then that they had those powers of creating forms of their own.

Now that you might understand, these entities were then, as you might say, thought forms, but were able to project themselves into material forms. Hence we would have these beasts, these living creatures that you would consider prehistoric, and many of those creatures that you would consider myths, or fables: the centaur, the satyr, the unicorn, the winged beasts, these things as have been drawn, things as have become from the imagination of man. All these things were beings materialized as thought forms. And as these Sons of God became caught up in material things about this earth, there were projected through them these grotesque beasts and things lower than the Sons of God, as these entities became.

This then was the reason for the first Adam. For it would be seen that God sent His Son into the world to take charge of the world and subdue the world. For it is spoken in your book of Genesis that this was God's command to the first Adam: Be fruitful and subdue the earth, as it should have been translated. Then we would see that the one ye call Jesus had entered as thought form on that land as you would call Atlantis and was known there as Amelius.

Other souls, soul entities, entered the beasts and mutants (as they might be referred to that had become grotesque and out of hand). Christ then came that these might be released from the earth and that that higher order of primates which had been evolved might be taken as a means of expression for these, that these soul entities might inhabit the flesh forms that were the higher of the primates, and in doing so might walk the earth with an intelligent mind.

What we now refer to as the conscious mind was given then as the third part, as might be said, of the soul entity, and was thus given this opportunity to live a life on this plane, on the earthly material plane. In such a manner they might be purified and gain, regain God Con-ciousness, and realize that their soul entity, that which they are, is God. Then once again they might identify with God and in bringing their soul entity back to that level, their thought patterns, their actions, these things might be purified through life on this plane. They would be given that chance to raise themselves back to the level of God and thus once again become one with God and know those joys, those pleasures that were theirs before the beginning of the world.

You have asked then if all these were once Sons of God and in what special way is Jesus, the one who became Christ, especially the Son of God, or known as His first begotten. We would see then that the Christ, as were all souls, was in the beginning with God, before creation and during creation, and through creation, and nothing was created without Him. This entity then was sent especially to earth as a higher form, as closer to God, as the one chosen by God to be His first begotten in fleshly form. Therefore we would see that He entered the earth at a higher plane.

Now how can it be that the Christ, that one who was perfect, would have sinned in the garden? We would see then in this manner: [for that] one who entered on this plane, a fleshly body yet still was God, there was not the possibility for sin, for this was foreign to God. But because it was the purpose of this man Jesus, entering this plane in order that all others might be given that chance for redemption, Jesus had to lose the God-identity, which was part of his nature, and become identified with man. Hence, the analogy of the tree of knowledge of good and evil and the reason for him and his soulmate partaking thereof. We would thus find that the one who tempted them was another entity, like as we are, but one who had fallen. Christ partook of this fruit that He might be complete man. This then was the purpose of God, the knowledge of God, that the first Adam might make it possible that in the last Adam all might be redeemed.

Then to further answer your question, there were with Christ, through His direction, the other Sons of God that came and materialized in the world at that time in five different places, in five different nations. Simultaneously the earth was inhabited. Hence, the five different races on the five different continents, if you would.

Now these were children of God. These had not lowered themselves through the creation and the frolicking in the bodies of the beasts. They came here that those who were so earth bound might be released.

Now this you will find in your own scripture if you read it carefully. All of this then might be realized through those words ye have recorded in your Bible. Then we find that from the beginning, those Sons of God who still were on the plane with God were given charge by God of protecting those entities that had fallen. We would find then that even in this day there still are those charged on this plane with aiding and seeking to help those of you who would raise yourselves back to this plane, and through growth, through spiritual growth, through evolvement, through cleansing the body and the soul, come back to be one with God.

#2406 (3-21-72)

EXCERPT 7

We would consider that astrology began as the world began. That is, it began as awareness in those first entities that manifested on that which you know as the earth or within this plane of existence.

Now in order to explain or in order to understand that which would be the astrological science relating to these entities, it would be necessary that we present an entire discourse on the creation, or that which caused the world or the human life as you know it, or this strain of evolvement, to come into existence. But suffice it to say for the moment that those who came as thought forms in Atlantis and those who manifested in Eden, as the first to take this body, that is the vehicle of the higher primates, and to inhabit these bodies in the sense of being a physical manifestation, were aware of the relationship between themselves and the universal forces.

Now we would find that that which you refer [to] as astrology operates in this manner and was the awareness even at this time. There was no birth of astrology in history, for it evolved with man. For the awareness was there before the world began. That is, each position of stars in the heavens, each position of the planets, the relation of the bodies, the planetary or solar bodies to one another, were the pattern of that which manifested under that influence. That is we would see it in this manner: The positions of the heavenly bodies as aspected to one another – not just the eight planets that you use or those bodies that you now consider in erecting that which you have called the horoscope chart but ... all bodies in your solar system – are a pattern of the bodies through which you manifest.

It was understood then by those who came into manifestation on the earth plane that the vehicle that they chose to manifest in was a carbon copy of the position of these various bodies in the heavens at the moment of inception, or that moment in which the soul came into the physical body.

We would further explain the same concept in this manner: That as an atom is the tiniest part of the human body, so the planetary body or the heavenly body as you would see them are part of a larger body. And as they move through this larger body, they form aspects, angles, relationships one with the other.

Now see the universe then as one large human body, for purposes of example. And this would be given only metaphorically as illustration, that you would see that as this body or that moves into a certain position within this huge body ... there is this manifestation, this state of health, this state of character, this state of personality, because of the arrangement of the atoms, the molecules, the organs, the relationship of the body functions between one another.

Now if this manifestation, this movement which is a constant force throughout the universe were stopped in a single second, that which came into being in that single second would be a carbon copy in miniature of that which was the universal manifestation. This then was the original understanding of astrology and this was the manner in which it was used. As a soul would seek to manifest in the universe, it would see the universe as an overall picture and it would choose that moment when these certain bodies would come into certain aspects one with the other to give character to the vehicle through which they would manifest. Therefore the question as is recorded here: How old is astrology? It would be said it began before the beginning, for those very first souls that manifested were well aware of the relationship of the stars in the heavens to the body, the vehicle through which they manifested.

One of the problems in the original manifestation or that which was called the fall of man was that these superhuman bodies as might be called, or these parts of God, these creative forces who looked at these vehicles from these angles were not aware of that which would happen as they manifested through this smaller copy. Or, that is, they were unaware of the trapped condition within the body, or the inability once they inhabited the body to be aware of that which they were aware of outside the body. Coming into the body placed them under the limitation of the smaller copy of the universe. We would see then that this began as a study as a valid science on the continents of Atlantis and Mu. And it was in these situations the hieroglyphs were chosen. Now the hieroglyphs as were originally given were attempts to recreate the movement of this particular planet as was seen from the outer positions before the manifestation in the human body.

But for now we would deal with those questions [such] as the place and time that astrology as a science began. In this sense, we would see astrology as a valid science. That is, that these forces manifesting under a certain pattern adopted that pattern. As the pattern changed then in the universe, it became a law that those changes manifest as well in the human body that corresponded thereto. This however has not been constant throughout the evolutionary history of man. For it was given of God that man should have free will. Therefore he was freed, as he practiced his will, from these astrological influences, thereby nullifying some of the laws of astrology, thereby ceasing that which would be a valid science, had it not been for the interference of the will of man.

Now we would see that as manifesting in this manner. That those aspects of astrology would rule a man's life if they were left unattended, that is, if man's will was not exercised.

That which was given as the will, however, is the most powerful influence in the universe. And even the stars in their paths can be influenced, that is, can be thrown off track, can be moved to different aspects between themselves by the exercising of the will in the smaller aspect or the smaller copy, the miniaturized depiction of the universe. The vehicles then can change that which it is the manifestation of, by the will of man. This was demonstrated by the Christ force, for the manner in which He lived His life changed the positions of the stars in the heavens and thereby created the end of the old dispensation, the beginning of the new.

Now there has been questioned whether there was a difference in Him who became the Christ, and those others of the masters who seemed equally as great. This then would be the answer to that question. That never has there been another who by living his life ended one dispensation and began a new. This has only been done by Jesus, the man of Galilee who became the Christ.

There have been other masters who expressed the Christ force and thereby brought salvation to their people, and brought example to their people and were great in every sense, and it is being given from these planes that we should not encourage that these be separated or thought of as different or one greater than the other. But they all are one, they all are the manifestation of the one force. It is only that this one brought a new dispensation.

This will occur again in that which has been called the return of Christ, the Second Coming of Christ, or the return of the Christ force. This will come not through the manifestation of a single man, but from the attuning of the hearts to the Law of One. When the Law of One is expressed, that is, made manifest in the hearts and lives of men – that is, when the will, the soul, the purpose of man is brought to one – the planets will line up one behind the other and express the Christ force in the world. This will be the second coming of the Christ, and the man from Galilee will appear and be made manifest throughout the world at all times, in all places, at one time. This will be the expression of the Law of One, this will be the bringing together, the ceasing of the duality between God and man. This will be the ending of the ages, the ending of the earth as you know it, for this will be a higher manifestation of all that is.

Now these are the laws of astrology, these are the laws of God. These are the constant universal laws. And these are the expressions of the Law of One.

#3002 (10-19-72)

EXCERPT 8

[There was a civilization] existing in those times more ancient than you have record or knowledge [of], in the southern portion of what is now California and western [parts] of Mexico. Now it [is] here called Lemuria or Mu, [and] this one [was] in the portion of Mu known as Lemuria, in those times when there came the height of civilization, the development of science, of technology here. We find among these peoples a period in which there was the departure, the rebellion, from both that natural law or that known or understood as God's Law, and that created by man, or those laws set down as morality or recognized as such.

Now in the developing of man and in the pride that came from development, or the feeling of accomplishment – as there was the developing of such instruments as would prolong the life, as would control the weather, and produce such effects for weaponry and practices of medicine, control of disease and such – there came the pride in the race, or among those peoples a feeling that they had grown above the necessity of moral law or a moral code. There came a time when such were given to adultery, and this became common. There was not the respect for the sex of the body and the use thereof and the purposes. There was open defiance of such given as morals and respect one for another and the worship.

Now these conditions set about conditions of the atmosphere or weather and that that surrounded the earth. Now in that day – and it remains true to this – that that system by which the universe was set in order and began to operate was perfect. And it would continue to be so in that day and in this if conditions were not tampered with by that imperfect or that less than perfect. That is to say there never would have been the shifting of poles upon this planet if there were not the creating of conditions among men that were defiant to the Laws of God. But when those conditions of law were subverted among men, and there was the defiance of the Law of God, so there was set in motion upon this planet an energy that created an imbalance between those forces of good and evil or of positive and negative ... Understand then that the movement, the shifting of the poles was caused by the activity of men in defiance of their God.

#8030 (8-11-73)

EXCERPT 9

Now this is Poseida [Atlantis], and this is fantastic. It is like a different world altogether because there are flying machines all over. I see so many of them flying.

Now you were a pilot of a machine, a flying machine, that worked in this way. Now the power of this machine comes from two sources – that from above and that from the earth side. Now there is a magnetism from the sun or from the celestial forces that draws upon the ship, and there is a magnetism from the earth that draws upon the ship. And these ships operate by creating a balance between the two forces. The solar energy is used to counteract the magnetism of the earth. And the power that provides the thrust is on the nature of what we would call a laser beam, that operates through a copper conductor that runs in two long channels along the base of the ship. Now the ship would have a shape like a long cylinder – no wings – only these two runners along the bottom that appear as copper.

Now on the top there is a window of something like plastic or glass, but it is of stone, or more in the nature of a crystal. But the vision of the pilot of this ship is more dependent upon the screen that is placed before him, rather than a window of the ship. There are transmissions that are radio signals that appear on this screen in a manner similar to our television – but not in the same respect because those things that are in front of the ship or around the ship are reflected upon the screen without means of cameras, but through the sensitivity of the screen itself. It acts exactly as if it were a window, a curving screen that is like a disc in front of the pilot that reveals all that is in front and in an arc, so that part of what is to the side is revealed as well, though this is encased in the metal ship. It is not a window at all, but has a sensitivity that reacts to those things within – an extended visual range. And this is the nature of your work.

I see another unusual flying machine. I do not know where ... assume that this must be part of the Atlantean existence – this one-man craft. It is ridden similar to the manner of the motorcycle without wheels, but it has curved wings – that is the wings extend outward and curve downward at the tips, just slightly longer than a man's arms, maybe two feet longer on each side.

Now these machines are black. The legs of the man wrap around a cylinder which produces the propelling force, but I see nothing of fire or smoke vapor. This is an electro-magnetic force. It is activated by a copper core that runs about three quarters of the length. It ap-pears hollow in the back. It relates to another force on the other side, and they seem to develop some sort of polarity in relation to each other, to equalize pressure or magnetic force on both sides of the ship.

Now the body would seem to be in direct contact with this core that runs along the topside of the machine, and the body is lying upon the machine facing forward. The controls are operated by the hands and fingers on either side of the machine as the arms reach around the machine and forward. Now the protective shield in front of the face again is not transparent but would seem transparent from the side on which the operator reclines, for it has a sensitive screen that reveals images of that which it is approaching.

Conductor: Will we find these machines in uncovering Atlantis?

This I cannot know. They seem to be capable of going high into space, somehow with no harmful effects to the rider.

I see also monorails in operation, and the speed on these things is fantastic – no conception of what we have in operation today or even what we have considered.

Now I see a lot of equipment as electrical or similar. There is a lot of use of plastic materials similar to glass or clear plexiglass, heavy plastic. I see a cylinder that has a surface like diamonds and facets that are cut in the surface of the cylinder. It is large, and it is made of crystal, and it is hollow. Now the design in the facets of this crystal is formulated by a law of nature. Now there is a mathematical system that governs the diagram, the lines of these facets in this stone. It is a system that we have not yet discovered, that we do not understand. But it is one that we could see in a constant, consistent pattern around us. And this is the system that is repeated throughout nature. This is nature's arithmetic.

Conductor: Can you give the formula?

The formula lies in a simple equation: 6 by 6 by 6. And this cannot be broken down as yet. This is recorded and will be discovered in openings of the pyramids, both in Egypt and Poseida, as they are uncovered. There has been a guard placed before these secrets that does not allow that they be revealed until that time as one who has already been selected and is being prepared shall come – and in opening the tomb these will be revealed.

Now this equation is the equation of the snowflake. It is the equation of the stars in our galaxy. The equation is found in the distances of the individual planets from the sun. This has already been theorized. But that which is missing in the theory will be discovered when this one who was an initiate will discover and reveal that which has been recorded.

Now under this crystal there is a couch that is shaped similar to the human body, on which the body rests. And there is a plastic or a glass cover that is hinged. And this crystal through which the sun is focused upon the body is used for medical purposes – and more than medical because those tissues of the body that are degenerating with age or disease are burned through solar energy reflected by the patterns through this crystal and are rejuvenated and the body is kept in a younger state or restored to a younger state.

Now this crystal and the rays of the sun, in providing this solar energy, are used for a multitude of other purposes as well. For this is the one great blessing that was entrusted to the people of Atlantis. And this is the very blessing that was abused, and it caused the destruction of Atlantis. For it will be learned that this crystal was used in a devastating way, in error, in tampering with the extent of its power. For it was known that the angles of focus of the crystal in regard to the sun held potential for a much greater power than that for which it had ever been used or was even intended that it should be used. Despite this awareness, it was allowed to become focused in such a manner as to cause cataclysms, a thing such as earthquakes, those things that would normally be regarded as natural disaster, but were caused by the power of the focus of the sun through the great crystal.

Conductor: Was this the crystal that brought about the great devastation back about the year 2800 B. C.?

Farther back, much farther.

Conductor: Will this cause the devastation in the year 2000?

No, no ... Now this secret may be discovered, the equation as to the crystal may be discovered about that time, may come into use sometime about then. Yes, for I see it in use and I see the flying ships. Yes, very similar, very similar, but not the same. And the crystal is not used in the same way.

For in Atlantis the crystal represented a spiritual entity. The sun represented God. And it should be realized that the sun was not worshiped as such by those of Atlantis and Poseida. But the sun was used as a symbol of the living God, the one God. And the crystal – because it was used in relation to the sun, and because it was realized that this crystal was a divine trust given by God to be used as He saw fit, to be used in His will and for His purposes only, and for the aid and for the good of mankind – because of this, it became a religious symbol.

#2404 (3-8-72)

EXCERPT 10

Conductor: [You] will answer the questions and give instructions regarding my work on the physical plane, my creative service.

Yes, we have the body and those records and witnesses of the relationship with the universal forces. Now we find this one coming into incarnation from the realms of Mercury, where there was the gathering together of that which has been the experience of past in-carnations, that it might be analytically assimilated. That is, filed or stored in memory banks, in manners, which may be used in the development of mankind in this century.

For we would find that it would be the purpose of this one to apply those laws that would bring together the laws of physics, as you have called the study of the discipline, with those laws of the nature, or the Laws of God with those that would be the spiritual laws. For [while] it has been realized it has not been developed that there is interplay, inter-relationship between those that you would consider the spiritual laws and the use of spiritual energies, which would be the patterns of mathematical functions or mathematical equivalents. And it is not that this one would have the ability to work with the numerical values, but it would be seen that a part of the discipline of this lifetime would be the ability to cooperate with those who may assimilate these values and may interpret the numerical functions and bring these ideas into play.

That is to say that it would be given in this manner: that there have been gathered in this Fellowship three who were part of the building of that which has been called the Great Pyramid. It would be seen then, that these would cooperate together in the understanding of the powers inherent in the pyramidal function.

There would be one then who would have the memory, the inherent memory, of the power, the feel of the pyramid shape – particularly of that particular pyramid at Giza, and those underlying structures. It would be his purpose then, his value, to realize that that which lies below ground surface as the foundation is important to the field, the energy pattern, the power of the shape within the pyramid.

Now we would find in cooperation that one who understands the numerical division, that is, the volume, the values, numerically. And his cooperation with this one in construction would be essential in interpreting, in finding those levels that would produce complete power or would concentrate the energy of geometric shapes, as would be found in the interest of this one.

We would see then that these abilities, these gifts have been divided for a purpose, as all the perfect plans of God work according to purpose to all those that are called according to His name and to His plan. That one would be given one ability that would not function without the cooperation of the other, for the teaching of The Law of One. For the pyramid is of no value unless it be understood – that which is the peak of the pyramid or that which all power centers from, that would be the bringing of all energies, all powers together. For herein lies the power of the pyramid, as it centers on the God force.

Then where would be the comparison of that which has been referred to as the geodesic dome with that which would be the pyramid shape? We would see it in this manner: that both would bring into play great sources, great forces, great pulls of energy. The pyramidal shape then would concentrate that energy, bring it to a point, and point toward the Law of One. The geodesic shape or the dome would spread that energy that is concentrated in its center over a wider force-field.

Now if there is the turning back in the memory toward that crystal of Atlantis, mounted as it were on the pyramid, and focused through the pyramidal shape, there will be the understanding [of] that [device] for the spreading of the pyramid, or those crystals, those facets of the crystals, over the geodesic shape, [by which] there was brought into play the great healing service that would spread over a wide portion of the land. Where there would be the need to concentrate or to focus this energy, there was used then the pyramid shape.

Now in the study for this one, we would instruct that the pyramid shape would be studied. And that there would be located that level of The King's Chamber that would be the focal point of power … and that there would be constructed the geodesic shape with the pyramidal frame resting over it. For we would find these combinations in both those temples that you have called the Temple of Sacrifice and the Temple Beautiful. For though the exterior was the pyramidal shape, the interior was the ovoid, the egg-shape, the geodesic dome resting inside the pyramid, and herein lies a source of all power on your plane.

Now understand not only the structural values of these geometric shapes, but understand those laws that apply to them. For all are contained in the Law of One.

That which would be the purpose then and the application of the life of this one would be in interpreting, in discovering, in putting into practical use those laws concerning the pyramidal inch, the pyramid shape and power, and that history that is given, the history of initiation through the pyramids.

And we would find developing in this one, the ability to cooperate with others, not always to be the leader, but the one asking, the one seeking, the one cooperating in love. We would find the great need for discipline in seeking, in learning those things that are not easily available to the finger-tips, for there must be a great deal of research in this area, and the application of mathematical abilities, and the cooperation between persons.

See this all for a purpose – the development of the character or the personality or the ministry – for many will be reached [through] these developments and the use of these experiences.

#7010 (11-12-72)

EXCERPT 11

There will be cooperation with thee – someone who is an engineer and would understand your focusing of solar energy through crystal, that may be used in cooperation with the pyramid energy, [or] that is, the focusing of these energies not only for the building of tissues in the human but for the reversal of the aging process within the human.

Now these would not be the development then of these two who have come, but of those who would come into the life, having these disciplines, these interests. And as there is the development, the understanding in thee, of the natural ways of life as are being developed within and are the love of this incarnation at this time, there would be the understanding that these are the natural ways for the preservation of self and provision for self, particularly in this age of destruction, as we find earth changes coming.

Use these opportunities then to understand, to research and to teach those natural methods, particularly concerning the earth and the geometric energies, the patterns (as would be said of these energies), the practical uses. For the energies have been discovered, and there is awareness. There has not been brought in the practicality of the use of such energy, and this would be an opportunity for thee for this subject of experimentation.

Now it has been given and would be of interest to thee that even under the Great Pyramid, or that is, in the hall before it and below the Sphinx, there is even unto this day food that was stored by the Atlanteans from their culture – both fruits and preserves that would be edible even in this day from the use of pyramid energy used to preserve these living foods, and might ... [provide] the understanding that even in this day such energies might be focused and become useful in your time. Understand these then as the natural methods, the natural ways of life.

There is so much to be taught and there are books that await on this plane that simply need to be channeled through a receptacle – one who is of the disciplines of Mercury or one who has been described, one who might understand those messages that would come from within and record these on paper. For the books, the teachings, the disciplines are prepared already by the masters and wait on these planes.

Realize that all books are written first on inner planes, inner channels, through those who become receptacles on your plane and would give the messages from within, the messages of the Divine. So many here have given so much for the development of our understanding of the Divine and the various disciplines that would be the teachings, the paths towards the central realization.

There is so little time on your plane for the understanding of these as men count time. For there is much that need be realized, there is much that need come in the processes of evolution on your plane. And these disciplines must go on, this plane must be raised to higher levels. There is so much attempt on inner planes to reach channels through which we may speak, that we may manifest, that we may teach those on this plane those laws concerning healing, those laws concerning the natural development of the human, and realize that the time is finished when there will be the progress in scientific and automated methods.

On your plane there must be the turning to the natural methods. This race must prepare itself for living without those artificial disciplines that have been developed. Hence, we find those as this couple who have come with the natural desires and memories, the innate desire to prepare self for those days when that which comes as so many artificial methods—the machinery, the technology of your day will be destroyed. The earth will be devoid of that which you depend on in this day for sustenance. There will need [to] be the understanding of the natural protection of nature, of earth, of the mother God. This is the discipline then that would be developed in thee and would be taught, would be shared with others.

#3008 (12-15-72)

EXCERPT 12

This one then as a doctor in Alta, [was] given much to the use of those natural remedies or the bringing of the plants for the treating of the body and the building of same. He became interested in those instruments of the time and the life. And the sojourn in that time was prolonged some thousand years as you count time by the use of those instruments that would burn away those elements that caused that process that you know as aging, or the failure of those cells to replace – or the focusing of that crystal used for such purpose or those rays as would be known.

Now the significance then of coming in that time, in that manner, was the understanding of the Law of One in this heart – or that in the beginning of this time, in those early times, there was the giving of self and the knowledge of the earth and that which the earth produced. Given in dedication to repairing, given selflessly for building the bodies, yet in those times as there was continued sojourn or the replenishing of the physical and living through much and observing, there developed something of cynicism or a different attitude toward life, toward those who have been helped. Or as might be described, this one felt that much had been built of proper and good. And the time came then in the feeling, "I will look out for the self." And in the understanding, the wisdom accumulated by one so long in sojourn on the earth, or continuing so many hundreds of years, and with the experience, with the learning and the developing of technical advances even as he watched these in the development, so this one became lustful for power or personal power and began to use that power or understanding to manipulate the populace or to build centers around the self.

Now these then began to become understood by those about, or the priests, those of the friends involved in teaching the Law of One or in the service of the Father God. So began the dissension among them or having been so long a servant of the Law of One, this one then in those latter times or in the times of the breakup, began to see the power building of those of the sons of Belial and that which they sought to accomplish – or to control the populace. And seeing that, they seemed to have control, began to take sides with these, or that in power as might be expressed.

And so took within self, or as part of self or the consciousness or the karma, a portion of that responsibility for the breaking up of the land. For these, as the crystals, as the opportunities focused for the healing of bodies, so it was discovered that these could be turned as well for the manipulation of power or building power or for changing the weather and weather conditions, and so were focused for such purposes.

These machines then, as there began to be the understanding of the uses or the focusing of these rays, began to be used for so many different purposes, for the guiding of ships, for the elimination of the huge beasts and those animals that had responded so well to the atmosphere that threatened other forms of life on this plane, so they were turned for such destruction. And having learned then that such could be used for destruction the sons of Belial then began to apply these as weapons not only against the animals but against mankind. And so began the building of power.

So came the karma or the detriment from that lifetime. And as would be counted as if this were many lifetimes, there was great buildup, or learning much that never would be lost and could be regained, yet as well much damage was done in the giving of self for power play. For the selfishness and suffering has come in such from those times.

Now in that time, there was the walking together with the present mate through much of the sojourn or some of the early years, though not present in that final breakup. We would find her then in the intermediate time when those did not walk together, but incarnated separately or for different purposes, that she had turned to that land known or as might be described here as Yucatan, now in South America, in those highlands where there was the attempt to preserve those of the teachings, those of the records, and was one of those responsible then for the maintaining, the keeping, the storing of such records in that temple as might be found and this would be described as in the present as buried under the mountain then – that mountain being volcanic and containing a lake in the crater at the top, and could be located. Yet under this would lie a temple that would, that could be found and would be unearthed. And here you would find records of that existence and even the name there, for her name in that time was Soo Lan.

These coming then the more recent times to Maiava, that would cover that portion of country now as Montana, as Wyoming – that central portion of this continent, then occupied by the more advanced souls or the more advanced tribes, those having gone out from Atlantis and preserving much of the records. Now these may be found buried along the river there, those rem-nants of such civilization as were given. There were the buildings again even in this area of the mounds, not recognized in this time as pyramids, but the mounds or flat surface on the tops, yet with record rooms or chambers below.

Now in that time both were given to the developing of healing and teaching. Or that is, the teaching of survival in that time. For was necessary for those having survived and inhabiting those new lands or spreading, that there were those that might be called the teacher-priests. Now not that these would be given for purposes of teaching religion, but if you would understand, there was not that which occurs in this time or the separation of the secular and the religious. For all understood and were aware that the living of the life within itself IS a religious practice and cannot be separated. So that those who were the teachers and responsible for the advance of others in any form were as well recognized as priests or as subordinate to God and His servants.

So in this manner, both were male in that time. Both were teacher-priests. And purposes then were for the research, the development of the use of those plants as could be found about that of the local habitat. Or these coming as aliens, unfamiliar with the surroundings, then began to experiment and learn that which might be performed with the herbs and that that grew, those minerals that could be found in the area, and to train those of the natives, or those already located in that area that were of the black race and had come from Lemuria in the early times or were descendants of other Lemurians. So these were given for the teaching here and the lifting of that race and the bringing of civilization in that time, though not as successful as the spreading in some of the other areas.

We would find more recently these returning to that area only some century, some 150 years [ago], that these were with the tribes in that same area, or wandered to that area from the east as there was the advancement of those coming into this country. So these were driven to the westward and found that very natural that they should inhabit that locale or feel at home here or be attracted to this area, having come then from that area now known as Ohio and those regions, those environs – so were driven out and made the home then in the West in those environs that have been the earlier habitat.

Now again we would find these as in charge of the children or looking after. Now understand that was habit among those of the tribe that certain ones would be assigned to the keeping of all children and others both male and female would go out to the hunt. Those assigned then for the care, for the keeping of the children, were given as well those tasks as preparing the food. Now understand that in preparing the food, there was as well the preparing of the diet or the herbs, that given for purposes of medical treatment. So there was as well the responsibility for the doctoring, for the medicine, and for the training of the children in that time. Not that these would be the medicine men, for these would find here the separation of the religion from the secular as it began in the red race. Or that of the medicine man would be more recognized as priest, if you would understand his function more correctly or as priest-medium, or given those purposes of contact to spirits.

Now understand if you could study that action of the medicine man in these tribes particularly the Cherokee, the Iroquois and those of the Blackfeet and some of the Sioux in this area, these were very gifted in spirit and able to see and discern the auras. And you will find from their records that the mating within the tribe was allowed according to the matching of the aura. Or that is, the medicine man, he who was the priest within the tribe, would observe the auras of the male and female and observe that as would be given for balance, and perfect match was given. For there was never a time when these were separated through the argument, through the fighting. For this was determined from those colors, those vibrations about, and were set in such a manner and were blessed of spirits. And these were selected, or those who became the medicine men were those naturally developed and able to communicate with the spirits then, those who hovered about and were given guidance in this way.

So these developed in such ways, not that they were medicine men, but they were aware of such and studied and understood and were given to such development – yet the purposes here for the preparing of nutrition and the teaching within the tribe.

Now if you would understand that which should be developed in this lifetime, then look upon that which has been developed. Now we have given not nearly all of those sojourns in that plane – but those of application to this time, or should be drawn upon, should be developed. For here are natural tendencies within the both, or the understandings, the ability naturally to understand those properties of food and the application thereof – and has been much waiting here or directing or attempting to reach the consciousness with those instructions that there should be given the study of that you would call the naturopath, or natural medicine, natural remedy.

Give self, dedicate the self to the study, for there is natural ability here to understand and to apply same and can be of service to many, particularly in this time when there will be the ending of that practice of medicine as you know it. For many, the many will turn away from that that now is the practice both in the professional fields, the politics, in medicine, in science. There will be the falling away from the respect given to those having graduated from the universities, the institutions. And those seeking help, those seeking medical attentions will turn to those who operate in the more natural ways or the naturopaths, the osteopaths, the chiropractic, these who understand the function of the body and the integration of body and spirit.

Now study in such ways and prepare the self. Begin with those books that are written. Those writings that have been given, as that called Back to Eden, we find as excellent as given And those are being recommended here, from those of the tribe or those gathered who are the friends and the portion of the family who are gathered here and attempt to speak.

Understand their presence and be aware of those about, for they would seek to guide thee in these ways and will help to reveal that. Now there are many others that are given as instructions for dealing with or understanding those of the ground or those natural herbs that provide the medicine and food or the living of the land. Search these and become very familiar. For opportunities will come, and your purpose will be given that you would guide those.

Now as you have come through one calamity and one time of change upon this earth, so were you prepared to guide others through another. Or you have the experience then in dealing with that confusion that would occur when there are the earth changes and the poles have shifted and there must be the adjusting to new environs. So it would be invaluable that such ones as these would be available and would know that of medicine. Not of the application as in the hospitals in this time, for these will not exist, but the understanding of those herbs that might be readily found within the ground and the elements within the dirt itself and within the ground. Learn the applications of these for many, many,

many will be dependent upon you in that time when there is the falling away.

Now seek to be of service and seek to understand for you will need to know those natural methods of teachings. And you have been brought this way from afar off for the purpose that you might learn to teach. Not teaching children then, not developing the young ones. But would you understand and see that which you have been taught. For the method you have been taught will equip you to understand and learn and teach those as not familiar. Or that is, that you would teach the language, that you would teach systems of communication, that for which you have no points of reference. Or that is, it is the method of teaching you have learned, not the application, but the manner in which such are given.

Now understand, by giving such teaching methods to one even who speaks of a different language, see the application here. See the reason for being brought so far to learn such systems that you may deal with those unable to understand language and culture. So you may begin again then with that of the new root race, or those unfamiliar with life on this planet, those just being born and new to incarnation, not having evolved as you. So you would begin to teach these spiritual concepts, not in those words as given here, but in the simplicity. So you will begin to introduce them that they may begin to understand, for they would fall at thy feet and worship thee for that knowledge that you would have, seeming so far beyond.

And it would be written of you that these are gods from another world, come to walk among us and teach us of these planes. Even now as it has been written of those who taught in those times of Atlantis, of Yucatan, of the Gobi, these other places where these came in the ships then after the collision. So would you come in this time and give the self to those illiterate upon this plane, not knowing of existence and not being aware that there are written records anywhere on this plane. This earth will be in such state of destruction as you will return to teach that there will be found no books, no history. And those found upon this plane will be wandering as the animals. And there will begin again those times of setting up the marriage, the homes, the civilization. All of these will be the responsibility.

Now this would not come as you see it in this lifetime. Or that is, there might be the separation of consciousness from the body, or the returning in the more perfected bodies. But understand, there is not the separation. This is not separation. This is not as if you would die and be born again or reincarnate, but rather that you would, through those separations or through those changes, the transformation of earth, so would you be transformed as well or lifted to higher levels, and come back as beyond, or not as the same nature or same vibratory rate, as those occupying or the younger souls upon this planet.

Oh that there were words that we could express that which will be the task and will be given to so many in this way. But look forward not to those things that we would attempt to describe here. They are given limitations of language for the reason that the consciousness should not be sent to this point. But rather concentrate on that which is at hand or that which should be done in this time. Begin to understand those of the plants of this planet. Begin to respect the self, the body. Begin to learn then how to heal both in the physical body and to teach that of Spirit or to cause even young children to understand. And if you would give the self in this time, in this moment, even now to understanding the abilities of awakening the God-Self – or look upon the children for which you will be given responsibility, and as you see the children, and as you see the formative minds, the inquisitive minds here, how would you explain to these that they are God, they are indeed manifestations of the Father? Begin to study such ways. And as you become able then to explain to the little child and cause him to awaken to his true self or who he is, to cause him to understand the I AM principles, so then you will be preparing the self that would return in those days to teach those who are the adult or those who are the illiterate, those who have no written language, indeed no language at all beyond the series of grunts or the pointing here or there. For it will be among your duties, your responsibility to teach these to speak, to use such mechanisms and to begin to make the records.

Now understand how important, how very important to develop

all of you. This is not given only for two, but so much here that might be shared. How important to develop those talents in this time, for that life upon this plane or the evolution of this planet will depend on that which you retain within the self from having lived.

Look at the opportunities about. How few, how few realize that opportunity of being incarnate on this plane. If only your eyes could be opened that you could see as we see now, the many multitudes gathered here. And so many have been attracted because we speak. There are a sea of faces attempting and would try to give the message through.

We are trying to say, we are trying to communicate that which they attempt to give. And that message they would attempt to give is: "Oh that we had the opportunity, even as you now, to adjust to this planet and to use the opportunities, the experiences of this plane to impress the consciousness, to develop, for it is upon this plane that you make those records, those grooves, those impressions that become as history or as a portion of the soul – that you may come back in another time better equipped to understand, to teach, to heal this plane, to cause the evolution of earth. It is not a thing that is caused by forces unseen. It is you. It is those living upon this plane that cause the evolution of this plane. And that which you would accomplish within the body or within the consciousness as you walk upon this plane, it is this that would cause the evolution upon this plane."

Then see the responsibility for even the breath that you would inhale at this moment, for that which you think, that which you give, that which you purpose in this moment and set as the ideal, is that which would occur upon this plane. It is that that would justify that life which you have borrowed here. For you have borrowed these vessels, these vehicles that you have come from those planes from which we speak even now and walk for a time upon this plane. And you are given responsibility for that plane, for this ship on which you walk, that you may prepare it, that it may serve as the footstool of God.

See then that you were sent here as emissaries, as missionaries to evolve this ball of clay, that it might become the castle, the temple, that which was originally designed or created as the thought of God. Now understand even as you came from His mind, His thought, to that perfect planet, understand, all of you, it was that which you played with, that you toyed with in that time, that destroyed the perfection of this earth. It is that reason that you have the responsibility for re-perfecting that which you have destroyed.

You have opportunity even now to remake, to rebuild. It is that we would attempt to communicate from here. Now we are aware that those questions that have been prepared, that have been written have been given little notice yet, but there are those here that have spoken, and had asked to speak, that have been waiting so long and it is these who have pushed, and have been eager, have been anxious that these messages might be given and only after these be poured forth from the heart of these who have come, so eager to communicate with their brother and sister here, only after they have been able to express could we proceed to those that are the questionings. We are prepared now for your questions.

#5022 (7-25-73)

EXCERPT 13

The wisdom that was gathered and became the products of the culture of those great civilizations – from Atlantis, from Lemuria, from the Greeks, from the Egyptians, the Chaldeans, and the wisdom of Israel – those things were gleaned that were gems of wisdom and were gathered in two great libraries. Both of these, the greatest, were located in Egypt.

In Alexandria the later collection of these was a storehouse of great knowledge. It was from this condensation of wisdom of many different cultures that those things were put forth that were the greatest of man's knowledge.

Now that which is commonly referred to as the wisdom of the ancients would be that course of study on the White Brotherhood, the completion of which was the initiation as has been spoken of, through the various levels of the pyramid at Giza.

Now this condensation of knowledge was stored and sealed at this same location. As has been given, it will be found in your lifetime. It is sealed and will be discovered in the arm of the Sphinx, which guards the pyramid at Giza. The secret which will lead to that chamber (this particular hall of records in the left arm of the Sphinx) is that it will not be entered from the passageway leading from the pyramid to the Sphinx, but through a subterranean passageway from beneath the left arm – the passage going back toward the body of the Sphinx, then up, then out again, away from the body. There will be found those guards, which remain there until the ending of their time, when the tomb may be opened. This is not to be confused with the record room in the tomb, for there too is a great storehouse of knowledge and relics of the culture of these ancients.

#2405 (3-19-72)

Diet & Health

Now we would give for these particularly that the diet should be vegetarian. In doing so we would suggest that it should be understood that it is not the difference that one discipline or another is better in the diet, except as found in the heart of the individual and his purposes in the incarnation. That is, one may be given as vegetarian; another may be given to eat meat. The differences then would be the type of self, the type of work, the type of development and the level of development for the particular lifetime and the purpose for the diet. For we would find, for those who are following the mystic paths and would be developing along the lines of understanding within, that the vegetable diet without the use of meat would be for the raising of levels of vibration. That is, the taking of meat or sweets within the diet or within the body would tend to bring those in spiritual development back down toward the earth plane, [or] that is, that there might be the conversing with others on lower planes.

Now it is often found that for a teacher there must be the two extremes within the diet. That is there must be the taking of the high spiritual foods. There should be the taking of the high spiritual foods. There should be the taking as well of the earth-bound diet, or that which would bring the entity back onto the levels of those whom he would teach. Hence we find that the vegetarian diet is not given to all who would develop spiritually, but [for] those who would separate themselves for the purpose of the refinement of self, the refinement of this incarnation. That is, [to those desiring] the release from earth in this incarnation, the finishing of the discipline in this particular plane of manifestation, would be given the vegetarian diet And it would be well for these, too, for the assimilation of that which would come as the discipline in this lifetime.

3008 (12-15-72)

EXCERPT 15

[In] Lemuria [there was provision] for the development here of plants or agriculture. Yet it would be so foreign to that which you see in this time as agriculture, for little similarity is given. For in those times were there the development of plants, or that is the putting together of this from this plant and that from that plant and creating the character in one. Or that is, there would be chosen the health of one [and] the beauty of another, that these be put together and produce that which would be taken for food. For all were given originally for food, you see, or in the entering in the earth plane, all things [existed] in perfection. All were prepared that one might partake of the other, yet [with] none losing the consciousness in the transformation or the acceptance of one into the other. Or that is, man understood that nature of plants and blessed them by accepting that which the plant would offer, giving of his consciousness in return for the health of the plant. So was there perfect sharing or understanding of the God nature. And if you be God, could you not bless the plant even as you take of its fruit so that He would bless you?

2030 (7-13-73)

EXCERPT 16

Now concerning the diet, it would be given: There must be more attention given to foods that produce energy, that maintain levels of energy, that sustain supply of nutrients to the body, particularly gelatin for the hair and nails of this one, and for the assimilation of vitamins in the proper manner. There should be taken a great deal of fruit juice, or fresh fruits in this diet. There should be taken no pork, and very little beef. Seldom ever should there be taken beef in the diet of one who is not particularly active. When there are the periods of activity in developing the dance, there may be taken then the heavier foods at these times. The diet then should be light, consisting primarily of fresh vegetables, fresh green vegetables. There should be taken such things as raw spinach. The leafy varieties of vegetables should be the mainstay of this diet, and for others in similar types of activity. For these will bring energy. These will bring spiritual energy and spiritual development within the body, and [will] attune the body to these purposes.

6005 (12-16-72)

EXCERPT 17

Conductor: What are the effects of simple sugar and refined starches on the physical and mental well-being of people in the world at this time?

Now these, we would find, attack and destroy nerve fiber or those nerve endings, particularly the ganglia around the spine, and cause as might be described a dross, or a flab, or inert cells to be formed within the brain tissue, thus hampering that that might be developed, or that might be given, slowing those impulses from lobe to lobe, from center to center, that there might be the clarity of thinking. These should be eliminated in all cases from diets, all refined sugars [and] starches. For much of value is destroyed by the taking of such. And particularly the cane sugars would be considered even poison in the system. Much damage [is] being done, particularly to the thought processes and the nerve endings, by the taking of such into the systems.

Conductor: Was the diet of the Atlantean civilization similar to ours at this time, and [if so] in what way?

In no way similar. There was the much giving to such that you might describe in this time as the whole grain wheats, and such fruits as dates, as figs, as those more darkly colored and a great deal of seeds. Little comparison with that diet that we see in this time.

There was as well a great deal of seafood. Little meat was taken if ever in such diet of Atlanteans, until the moving to the new world. Not until that revolt against beasts, when these were attempted to be destroyed by the gathering of nations, was there the taking of meat into the diet. This [was] late in the development of earth's atmosphere. This [was] considered even cannibalism among those inhabitants of Atlantis and Mu.

1040 (4-13-73)

EXCERPT 18

Conductor: My husband has had symptoms of heart disease or tension. How can we be sure which it is?

Yes, we have this body. Now we would find these indications of pressure and pain as coming primarily from the diet and from tension. There could be produced and will be those conditions affecting the heart if these are not corrected. Primarily for this one, there would be the less taking of the cooked fat, or that is, fried foods, or any foods in which the oils or fats have been heated, for this causes the breaking down of elements within such oils.

Now the oils taken into this system should be pure vegetable oils such as olive oil on the salad, but never heated or cooked. There should never be fried foods, never any pork in this diet. Bacon may be taken well fried and well drained. There should be taken more of the fish and fowl. These as well should be taken without the fat and never fried.

Leave off vegetables of the pod variety from this diet. There can be taken cabbage if cooked or steamed, but never raw. Should be taken a great deal of lettuce. Careful to chew this well, for the roughage would produce a problem within this system, particularly in the lower intestinal tract. When there are taken, those vegetables that contain seeds, for this diet remove as many of the seeds as possible, particularly those seeds that do not digest. There would be a problem with the assimilation of corn for this reason. And take a great deal of the dark green leafy vegetables for this diet, with little seasoning.

The correction will come then in the attitude, the settling within. Would be well for this one to set aside a time three times daily when there would be the quiet time within. It need not be called meditation, but it need be the resting, the allowing the body to assimilate those foods that come in. And cause the mind to file away those thoughts, those disturbing factors of the day. It is simply for health that the body should be still at regular intervals and allowed to assimilate and sort out those factors of the day that would produce this type of tension and gas within the system.

This one need not suffer heart trouble if there is care taken in the diet and in the attitude. See that there are the restful times. Program the body to be relaxed and rested.

Conductor: How important is fasting?

This of course is an individual consideration. We would see, however, there would be few on your plane who could not benefit from the cleansing of the body, the mind and the spirit in a period of fasting, in a period of dedication, devotion to the Divine. The attunement of self for most on your plane would require this period of fasting, and we would see it entered into in an intelligent manner; that is, that you would care for the body. See the conditions of the body and the ability to provide for the body, to sacrifice, to cleanse. See these as all occurring for a purpose.

Set aside a period of time that would be adequate for the fasting. It would be well that there would be set aside three days for the cleansing of all who would seek to raise themselves to a higher level on your plane, which would be given to anyone who would be prepared to cleanse the body, the mind, the spirit, and attune to the Divine. Set aside three days where there would be taken into the system only raw apples and water. There could be taken prior to the time of fasting, vitamin supplements for the building of the system. This will be found, however, not necessary during the fasting itself, for the action of the apples would remove all food value from the system. The taking then of supplements would be of no benefit during this three-day period. After a period of three days, we would find that anybody taking the raw apples and water for this period would find the body completely cleansed within and without. Taking then at the end of the third day a half-cup of pure olive oil to flush these from the system, he would be found physically cleansed within.

Now it would be important that this be done then on all three planes at once. There would be the outer washing of the body with clear water and salt; that is, adding salt to the water and blessing it, doing this for spiritual purpose as well as physical cleansing. Spend the time then sorting out mentally, for the cleansing of mental planes. Cast out of the mind that which is the thinking process, cast out all that which is not needed, that has not been assimilated. All ideas, all concepts should be cleansed from the mind, even as there is the flushing from the body symptoms of that which has not been used. Do the same then during this same period with the mind. Flush from the mind all those concepts, all those ideas that are not needed and are not productive. Particularly guilt and fears should be flushed during this time.

On the spiritual level then, seek attunement and seek the filling with light. As there is brought into the life the light, the pure healing light, the cleansing light, the purple ray of the Father, so would there be the fasting, the cleansing of spiritual planes.

Now realize that it is not possible that such phenomena could occur on your planes without the Tempter working as well. See what happened to the Christ, the Man of Galilee. Was He not tempted, even sorely during this time? And would you not be on your plane as well? Realize that during these periods of time there would be the aggravations, there would be the temptations to turn from this way during this period. These would be seen as spiritual trials, even as physical trials occur.

It would not be possible that you would dedicate these three days, giving yourself to raising self to higher levels and attunement to the Divine, without superb results. We would see all who would be so willing becoming divine servants of His and ministers of the Gospel throughout the world. And through so doing would raise your entire race a little closer to the Godhead. Seek to be of service in these ways, for there is much needed that needs be done in this day for the attunement to the Divine.

1007 (12-1-72)

EXCERPT 19

Now there is much that needs to be channeled for this one. And there needs to be the energy of all in presence, that all these instructions might be given in this single time, that this one be sent forth with a mission upon this earth to express the Christ, and to cause men to come to awareness in this day and prepare for His coming.

So then there might be brought those disciplines of yoga, or the physical exercise, the attention to the physical body, that this one might take the fingers, and the awareness, and touching the various portions of this body daily.

Now set aside a time, a particular time. Do this rhythmically, so that the same portion of time is set apart with each day for the purpose of development, of dedication of these muscles, these nerves, these sinews, these tissues, these bones for the purpose of Christ. Then perfect this body. Speak to the portions of the body saying, "I am God. Be still and express the perfection of God in this body." Speak then to the gland centers, to the nerves. Honor this body as the temple of the Holy Spirit, and so perfect it.

And when there would be brought the food into the body, look upon what you would take into the body and see this as that which you would add to the temple of the Holy Spirit. "And [so] would these windows, would these doors, would this material with which I build this body of the Spirit reflect that which should be the temple of worship or the expression of God in this world." If you see not the food then as an expression of God, or that which should be given to the expression, the perfection, of a temple of God, then take it not into the body. But as there is the taking, then so dedicate it that it would express only truth, only purity and beauty.

So would not a physical vehicle be perfected even in this day? Even as you gave of the service and were given as a minister for the purpose in that day, of perfecting those animalistic bodies and bringing them into perfection in that day. So would you not give self to the purpose of dedicating this body in this day? So would not God channel His perfect message through a perfect body?

Now it is not out of the realm of reason, or understanding, or acceptability, or believability that you could express then through a perfect body, even though this one be so out of balance in this time. Is it not because of the indications of lack of discipline brought into the time, into the exercise, into this life? But set apart a portion of each day, each period being dedicated for its purpose. Know that each hour of the day belongs to Him and should be dedicated for His purpose, to be set apart to some act of God. Then set apart thy day in such a manner. And breaking it down into the 24 equal parts or portions, express in this portion that which should be expressed of the Christ for this portion of the day. That which would be the expression of Him, that which is appropriate to this portion of the day, would be expressed. Then so use thy day, thy body, thy life, this earth for the perfection, for His purpose.

Know that the time is short. The vibrations of this earth are being raised to such a high level that those who are not in tune with His purposes, with His import, with His message, cannot remain upon that portion of the earth that would be so perfected. And that portion then that would be destroyed, would your feet walk thereon? Then be lifted. Be lifted with His church. Be caught up to be with Him. If it would be so, then perfect the self, the body, the mind, the spirit. Show forth His life as you would walk your feet upon this earth.

Now this one might further understand – as there would be the setting apart the schedule, the giving of self in these ways, for such perfection – that there might be brought those proper balances within this body. We would see that there should be the daily taking of the gelatin, so that which is taken could be better put to use within this body. Take much less of the salt within the foods, using only the sea salt, or that naturally developed, not those crystals, not those chemicals as normally given, but using sea salt and using very little thereof. Taking daily then the alkaline substance, particularly the juice of lemon or grapefruit for such balance, and in the taking of a great deal of lettuce and the fresh green leafy vegetables. There needs to be taken much less of meat or meat products, less of that which would be sweet or pleasurable to the body, that there might be developed the discipline of the body. That which would cry out for satisfaction in these ways should be subdued gently, becoming the master thereof. Study then those things that have been brought concerning the diet and the proper balance in these manners, and be disciplined in this way.

Now if you would express then that which should come in this ministry – and this is not given only for the artist but for all who would come – so discipline the life in this manner that that which you have set about to create in this lifetime, that which you ask for opportunity to do in coming into this body, into this temple, might be done. So then might your feet walk even as His walked, so you might be caught up on the clouds to be with Him as those changes would take place. As this earth would be seen as a piece of clay in the hand of the Master – that it may be crushed, that it may be reformed, remolded – might not that vessel that would express further the beauty of God be pounded first into that ball of clay, then flattened, then brought into perfect shape by the skilled hands of the Master?

See then that this earth, not for punishment, but for perfection, would be crushed then beneath the heel of His hand. Those then who have prepared themselves, have become the vessels, the instruments, would they not be caught up even in the ethers then waiting with Him, becoming then the bride of Christ, marrying self? And in the marriage, would not the two become one? And as this ball of clay then again is set spinning in its portion of the universe, then would your spirits, those that have been perfected, gather about it then, bringing a new Heaven and a new Earth.

Oh that we might lift the scales from your eyes and see that which we look forward to, even on this plane. And there is here such anticipation, such longing. And so many have gathered in this presence at this moment seeking that we urge you that you would express Him, His vibrations, even now the perfection, that then there might not be the waiting, but that the Son of God would come in the clouds. Even so, come Lord Jesus!

Then allow that that day might come now, for there is untold beauty waiting to unfold, that might be expressed through you, if you would so give self to His expression. Then, be it so. See the beauty that would awake if there would be the expression of the Christ in this world in this day.

#3016 (2-25-73)

Healing

Now we would see development of healing in this manner: As there is developed within faith and love, so healing comes as a natural result; would be seen in this manner, that one you would love enough to give all that you have to make whole, perfect, and well, there is then the exchange of energy that would produce healing within that body. Healing essentially as you would see it, that is, magnetic healing on your plane, is a development of energy and can be assisted, can be aided, can be produced in deep breathing when there is the attunement. That is, all energy that is needed, that is necessary for accomplishing any task on Earth plane exists within the atmosphere of Earth.

There are elements, there are energies, there are powers in the atmosphere of earth that man has never yet dreamed of having tapped. These can be tapped, however, and used and have been by those who were the saints of God, for centuries, in the manner that they realize that all work according to the divine law of God, and that in attuning the heart, the mind, the spirit, with those divine laws, all these energies may be tapped and used.

We give then that there is available, even at this moment about the body, all the energy that is necessary to build and heal tissue. Then, all that is left is the directing of this energy. Be aware then, that there is no direction of this energy without the attunement of the Divine, without the use of the Divine Law. Become then

channel. See self as a channel. Realize that what you have been given, that is the body centers, those centers you call chakras, or the kundalini force, is but an electrical conduit from this divine energy that fills the atmosphere with the prana of life. Use this as a conduit between self, between God and the one that you would heal.

Raise these levels of energy, then, through deep breathing, through the filling of the lungs with the prana of life. Now, when there is the practice of the deep breathing, see that you are taking in not only air, not only oxygen and those elements that have been discovered as a part of the atmosphere, but see, be aware, open your eyes, and realize the fantastic energies that pulsate, that swarm even now about your body. And, as you breathe deeply, realize that you take in all that is necessary for the healing of any body on this plane. See no limitations. Accept no limitations. There is no disease that you could not heal if you would accept that proper energy into the body and channel it into the body of the one that you would seek to heal. Know that all He has done you can do and greater things even than the Christ Himself did on this plane can you do in His name as you only will claim this power and channel it for His purposes.

1007 (12-1-72)

EXCERPT 21

Yes, we would take the son in this moment. We find this as being still and rested. We see this injury as affecting in this manner: that there is a pocket on the lining of the lung that would be filled as it were with air, for lack of a better expression. But we would see that there the pocket did not reseal after there was the infusion of lymph and liquids in this area given for the healing. Now the reason that this is not drained and closed or healed in that there was constant activity of the lung even at this time, and the pressure built around this healing process was interpreted by this seeker as pain within the body. That which should have been interpreted as pressure was interpreted as pain, which is common in the body processes. Now the presence of pain therefore produced tension, causing the greater pressure.

We would see then that which results at this time is not the injury, but the result of an injury; that is, the problems that persist would be psychosomatic. If there would be the release of pain, the release of tension, the release of fear, then the releasing of the tension and fear would release the pain, for this is a cycle, and one would propagate the other.

We would see that there would be one of two methods that might be used for the release of this problem of the lungs, and it should be released for the reason that this tissue could turn to cancerous growth or infusion of cells, improper cell growth if not dealt with. The one method would be to collapse this lung, using then the other lung to carry the weight as this one would be given opportunity for healing.

We would see, however, that this would not be the best way and [it may] be corrected ... in this manner: that one who is close, one who particularly loves this one, would form a bridge with the hands that is a force field. She may be seated at a table or other surface where the tips of the fingers would be put together to form a bridge or a pyramid. Then there would be seen the son and the conditions of this. . . that is on the lungs, his injury would be seen as resting in the base of this pyramid. The loved one then would enter into a time of meditation and attempt to produce warmth within this force field or within this pyramid. Now see this warmth as being the light of God. See the warmth as being Creative Energy. See the warmth as being heat that would flow into the chest cavity and produce healing, would drain away the tension, would drain away the wetness that would prevent these two layers of tissue from closing and fusing and healing again together. See then the edges of this scar tissue fading away, fading into healthy tissue.

Now as there is the programming in this manner daily without comment to another (no one else need know that you are doing this effort, for the calling of attention to it by anyone else who might doubt would drain off energy) there needs to be built the force field of belief. Lack of belief on the part of anyone who would know of this would drain away the energy of belief. See then that this would be between self and God, calling on God then to produce healing in this area, and we would find that the spot gradually would fade away from the edges to the inward, and as there is the rechecking in a few months and the X-rays taken, this spot would be found to have reduced at least half in size and there would be the additional faith from the seeing of the Hand of God at work; would be the increased effort then and [the injury] would fade away completely and would produce complete health.

It would be seen then, that there would be within the heart the great desire to share this with the son, but this should be some years from now rather than at this point, for there will come a time in this one's life when he will need to know of these things, for there will be the use of the power of God in this life for others. If given now would not mean so much. Ponder these things in the heart then. See and realize the hand of God and cause it to be a part of the life.

1007 (12-1-72)

EXCERPT 22

Conductor: You have before you (22002). Please comment on past incarnations that would affect career training and study in this lifetime.

Yes, we have the body and those records and witnesses of the relationship with the universal forces. And we have this one coming from the realms of Saturn where there is the satisfying of those karmic relationships in this lifetime.

It has been given that this one should be the teacher. There is much development that must come in these areas, but the concentration in the studies for this time should be upon the teaching. The creative writing would be well to study, though this will not be the field of this one. However, there will be a book written by this one concerning the healing processes on the body and the means of teaching same. These would come as we would see as they develop in the individual; that is, these are not given as the effects that will be but the possibilities of that which can be, for there would be the development first in self.

Now we would find that that which comes as karmic relationship for this one lies primarily between this one and the channel through which we speak. It would be given in this manner, that this seeker was the teacher and the healer in those early days in the Egyptian existence. And this one who is the channel had come before her for the healing and there was lack of belief in this one that these could be accomplished. There were the long periods of time and the moments of agonizing prayer for the seeker concerning this channel and others as well not only this one through which we speak. And it was the great difficulty of this lifetime of healing to bring about belief in those bodies that were attempting to be corrected from the more animal states to the human, as we would see the bodies being perfected. And there was the choice, then, of this one, that there would be the returning in these relationships that this one then would suffer that which he saw being suffered by those in the healing relationships, or that is, the process is being reversed. Then the belief must now be aroused in this one.

Now we would have you see the situation in this manner: that the difficulty here was for the healer to understand the difficulty of those being healed, in believing that these things, these appendages as tails, the hooves on the feet or the claws or whatever were the manifestations of that which was not quite human there must be aroused in this beast form the ability to believe that this may be corrected so that there might be the progress [through] the arousal of faith within these. The frustrations, then, of the healer became the negative forces, the negative vibrations producing the cause of karmic effect then. This is not entirely a negative, or loss. It is come in that this one might produce for the others the opportunity of that which she had. It could be seen then, as a beautiful relationship; that is, that this one as a healer was so thankful for the opportunity of being the instrument that she would share with others this opportunity of this lifetime. See this then, as the purpose for coming into this lifetime in these manners that there might be the demonstration for all those so afflicted that these can be overcome, that mind is the builder, that new bodies may be created through the mind.

Now before giving those that would be the disciplines for these corrections or health problems we would answer that question as has been given concerning the studies and developing of those that would be the talents. Now the art, of course, should be developed and there is the great ability in this area, and may be shared, may be used, particularly in that question as was asked concerning the Fellowship and the center. Both these places might do well with some of the art if this art expresses the innermost feeling of this seeker toward that particular place. That is, what do you see in that center, what do you see that it needs, what do you see as its expression? Put this on the canvas and seek to create a healing atmosphere. Seek to create something on the canvas to which those who come seeking would react, and would be blessed in doing so. See this then, as the creation is made see it as a ministry for this particular purpose. Then study those subjects as would be necessary for the teaching particularly for the teaching of those who would need the correction of the limbs or the use of the limbs in manners such as occupational therapy. Prepare self, then, to do the teaching, the public speaking, the writing, for this will be the service of this one for which she will be remembered.

And realize ever that healing can come. We would see it in this manner, that there would again be taken those who would be the healers, who would share in this opportunity. And we would program this mind to correct all those impressions as have been given. That is, it would come in this manner: that there is throughout the day constantly the reinforcement from all those about her. One only need cast the eyes on the appearance of this one, and there are the immediate reactions saying "This cannot be healed. This will not be corrected." That is, all of the vibrations that this one meets in the eyes even of strangers are the negative projections saying "I can't— this can't be done."

Then we would seek those who are the members of this Fellowship and those who would be the healers, those who would work with this one would reverse this atmosphere. Now this being a 24 hour a day proposition the answer then will be given 24 hours a day; or that is, there will be the cooperation between these members that this one would be helped in the thoughts, in the creativity of the mind: one taking each hour throughout the day and there would not be the ceasing of the times when positive projections are made toward this one. Or see it in this manner: as one would take the period from 7 to 8 p.m., and during this hour would see this seeker as being whole and complete. See her as being active. See the body walking, see the body playing the sports, see it in all manners as perfect and corrected.

Now as you are led to believe that these things may be done, they will begin to manifest. And how will they begin to manifest?

First of all there will be the reprogramming in this seeker's mind. There will be the beginnings of belief, for there is not now even the beginnings of belief that this is possible. But it will be programmed into this mind that which has been constantly programmed as negative not by the family, for we see very positive influences in this family, those close around her but in the daily activities there has been the constant negative programming. There has not been the belief that this can be corrected. And it would be thought by some, even to be said in her presence at this time that it can't be corrected.

It would be said that we are creating false illusions, giving false hopes. And as long as that is believed, as long as this is projected, it will be true. But we see this as not being necessary, and we see those in this Fellowship as being able to realize that this is not necessary. And we see this as the entire mission of this group: that there would be the reprogramming of these thoughts in the many cases. There will be the proof of the power of God, on this plane of Earth as you see it today. It is time this day for the perfecting of God's laws and then seeing the demonstrations of the power of prayer at work. Now how many hours a day would the negative influences put in working against this, so let it be for the positive influences. Be not the one to break the chain, or it would be better that this not be started at all.

22002 (11-1-73)

EXCERPT 23

Conductor: You have before you one (3001). You will give advice as to how this one might enlighten himself to the Christ forces within him and how he might learn the lessons that need to be learned for the best usage for himself at this time and in this body and this mind.

Yes. We have this entity and the records of the relationship of the universal forces. We would find one coming into this lifetime from the area of Venus, whose need in particular is to express love and to be a catalyst that would cause this expression or give opportunity for this expression in others. Now we would find in this mind that it has come to this one that I will not receive those indications that that which has come into this life has come as a result of karma, or that is, that this one would say it would be the pat answer to say that I have done this or that in a past life and am being punished in this life through those conditions in the physical body, and I do not see that as being the conditions under which I exist.

There would be the preference, then, that this one would be told that this manifestation is for the purpose that (as has been said) the Son of God might be glorified, or that this is a mission, this is an opportunity for advancement in this life. Now, we would have this one see that both are true. It is not a choice of either one or the other.. First of all, that karma is not punishment, but opportunity to meet a situation that is necessary for growth. Never should karma be considered punishment. All punishment that comes into the human life or into the human soul, into the human existence, is brought by the entity himself, or that is, by the soul himself. That one who would judge self is self. The punishment then is that so much of what is accomplished in a lifetime is discarded, is cast off, to the areas of Saturn where it is burned and remembered no more: that is, that only those positive things, the positive building, remains with the soul and goes on to be a part of the soul. All else is cast into the lake of fire to be consumed. This is the only punishment meted out to self that that which is created continue not with the person unless it is the positive, the building aspects. See then for this one (who has misused a past life and is expressing that in this life), that there needs to be the opportunity for growth, or the opportunity to use the body in a proper manner, whereas this was not done in a former incarnation.

Therefore the information will not be withheld from this one, saying that this (polio] is not because of something that happened in a past life, for it is true. It was a result of a misuse of a past life when this one was a dancer in the court of the king, Louis XIV. For there was for this one the much misuse of the body of the life. There was the much pride of self, there was much abuse of others, for this one had the tendency toward the sadistic expression of sex and produced in many young girls of the time the misshapen or lack of attractiveness in the body because of the mistreatment of the body of these ones. Now this would be repulsive to this one in this lifetime and indeed this would be understood that it should be so, for this is the growth process, this is that which needs to be adjusted to. Be thankful, then, for the opportunity to set aright those circumstances that were wrong. And those who will come into the existence in this lifetime will be manifestations of those who were mistreated in past lives.

What then would be the growth process for this one? It would be seen in this manner: that the ministry, the whole life, the work of this one would be to raise the consciousness level of those about him, and in doing so one's own consciousness level is raised a little closer to the Godhead; or that is, there is the closer attunement with the Godhead within self if this were inspired in others and given as opportunity to others.

Now how much faith would there be in this one? It is said that there are those who are manifesting in this lifetime, on this plane, with the physical illness or the misshapen limbs for no other purpose than that the Son of God might be glorified, or that is, that those who would practice healing, those who would want to be the healers, might be given the opportunity to express this in this lifetime. And we would find this, as well, expressed in this one that this is the purpose for manifesting in this body in this manner. But where is the faith? Is there the realization that these things can be accomplished? And would there be the attempt, not only for this one in this body, but for those who would call themselves the healers, or for those who would aspire to be the healers? And who is a healer? Is it not all the servants?

Now we would find then those about this one who should be of service to God in this manner. And if you would seek to serve, here is this opportunity, for this will take several hours per day each day, that these may be practiced. Now is it not possible that the God forces that created this body could set it aright spontaneously, or that is, that it could happen in a few minutes? We realize of course, that worlds were spoken into existence with nothing but the movement of the hand of God, and can be done. We would see, however, that this is not the manner in which God would seek to work in this, for would it not be the more benefit to the servants that through the application of self would come the growth? Would they not be taught patience? And would not indeed there be seen through the effort of these ones the building of tissue, the healing processes that would come? And we would see this occurring in this manner: that there would be at least six daily that would volunteer and would assist this one, that there would be the much prayer, that there would be the lending together of vibrations.

Now the most helpful influence for this one would be the attuning together of the six with self. Realize the significance of the number seven in this healing battery, as it would be called. For in the number seven and in the attuning of self together to the number seven, would be the realization of reaching a spiritual level. Now seek this as interpretation given in the book of Daniel: the dream of Belshazzar and the experience of that dream that the seven periods of time were the raising of the seven levels of consciousness. The higher level then being the spiritual level or that level of spiritual attainment, that level which would be called spiritual awareness, is what we would seek within these seven. And through this voluntary process and through the working together, that seventh level would be reached, not only in this entity who comes seeking, but in those who would work about him.

Now, we would have one, then, who would center the attention on the forehead: that is, that the tips of the fingers will be placed on the forehead of this seeker, and there would be the prayer, the at tempt, the programming from mind to mind of attempting to inject faith into this system, or that is, that the one placing the fingers would believe that this is being used of God; there is the attunement together to the forces of God, and they would be seen as sharing the energy from the prana of life or the perfect energy of God together, becoming one together. And the one placing the fingers, the hands on the forehead of this one would say in doing so:

"As I have health, so I give unto thee;

May God bring health into my body and share with thee.

May I have no more of health, no more of God

Than would be manifest in you;

That is, you and I are one:

Until you are well, I am ill."

See these things as sharing the perfection of God. Then we would have the others that would be working on the legs, and there would be the wet cell application of the battery that is, the wet cell battery applied to the muscles of the legs for this purpose. We would find that most of the muscles of these legs are intact, although there has been the removal of some muscular tissue and has been the rearrangement of muscular tissue in this body for purposes of leverage, and others that were done through the orthopedic works here on this body; and there has been some damage done that will not be completely corrected. However, these legs can be given use in this manner: that through the stimulation of the wet cell battery, there would be called to the, attention of these muscles that have gone to sleep; there would be produced the artificial reaction, or that which is not produced through the nerve impulses from the brain will be produced from the outside. That is, the muscles will jump or jerk or move or be programmed to move from the outside application of electronic impulse the same type of impulse that would come from the brain, though of a different frequency. And by calling attention, by calling attention of the body to these muscles, and by causing the body to realize the existence of these muscles, the body will be programmed to send better impulses to and from. There would be the stimulation, the manipulation, and there would be the programming of these legs in these manners, as if it were programming the brain.

Move these legs then in the manner that would be the normal functioning of the leg. Seek that each muscle would express itself as it should express, if the construction and growth were normal. There would be then the constant programming, the constant assuring. Speak to the muscles themselves. Speak directly to the muscles of the body and assure them that they are able to express themselves.

Now this will be a strain on the faith of all concerned. There will be the bits of doubt here and there that this even can be done. Therefore we would see that you would attempt this first, and attempt this together along with the other attempts that first of all, there would be the battery of prayer about the legs that you would produce the redness, the warmth, the warming sensation in the body. And seeing that this is done, seeing the power of prayer manifest will lift your faith a little more and will help to build power to believe that these things may manifest.

Now would it not be the shame that we would have to lead you by the hand in this manner? Are you not able to believe that what God has constructed He can reconstruct and bring to perfection? But lead your faith by the hand until it becomes big enough to walk. And in this manner you will see that you will build tissue, that you will exercise muscle, that you will program the perfect reaction of the muscles in these bodies.

Now we would seek cooperation from one who has medical training or would realize that which we would perfect in the anatomy, the physiology; and we see one, , who is a chiropractor, who may be contacted and will be happy to work with this one. There will be the objection of this doctor that he would say "I am the chiropractor. I work on the conditions of the spine and not orthopedics, or not the extremities of the legs and not this type of condition." We need not that type of physician but we need this one who is cooperative and has faith and has healing in the hands, for we see this as part of this one and we see in his mind the ability to attune self to meditation states and to the awareness of the God forces and the healing powers of God. We would have this one examine the body then, and see where the construction is not perfect and will see the areas or manners or the directions in which the patterning should take place. That is, this one will set up the programs of moving the legs in this direction and that, in the walking motion, in the standing motion, in correcting the positions of the bones as they should be.

Now that which is the habit of sitting now with the legs splayed, or that is, with the legs spread out to the both sides is not a natural position that is, the person whose legs have formed perfectly could not sit in this position. Observe, then, that which is the tendency of the person with the normal functionings of the legs, and seek to simulate these mannerisms in self. That is, program self to see the body as perfect. Construct in the mind, as it were, two mirrors, and see in the one as it now exists, and see in the other the body as it should exist. Examine the body carefully in this second mirror that is the perfect mirror and seek to construct that which you see.

Now as you pray believing that you already have received, it shall be given. Do not doubt the promises of God and remember, as was the saying of the Apostle Paul: "I can do all things, through Christ, who strengthens me." Now as you ask, so shall you receive.

Now those who would be the blessed and those who would be of service to God, let them volunteer, and this must be done daily. And remember this, for those who would be assisting in these programs:

It is better that a thing not be started at all than to be started and stopped. Be faithful in the service of God and as you give to this one so shall you receive in your own life. Now those who would see a miracle of God take place, let them volunteer, and through the volunteering and through the giving of their service to this one will come the greater spiritual growth. Has it been given, the greatest that you can do is offer a cup of water in My name? And who will be the more blessed on this plane that one who would preach to the thousands and ask for emotional reactions and concepts within the mind or those who ask not for glory but would seek to serve just one, one human being on this plane, and would give hours and hours of time and patience and love and faith and concentration and attunement in the programming of this body? As you would receive, so should you give.

3001 (10-26-72)

EXCERPT 24

Yes, we have this body and those gathered here, and that to be given was particularly for this body, and for the care thereof and for the instruction for those as would study the healing or prepare themselves that they might better understand and apply those laws of healing, and for this body we would continue the use of the liver, but cooked not with butter or oil but with a little water and onions, taking a great deal of this into the system. It would be taken as well for the strengthening of the system and the blood the preparation of the chopped dates and figs (those Assyrian or black dates or figs chopped together with a little corn meal) and the cracked wheat or wheat germ might be prepared with the goats milk, these steamed together with a double boiler and taken two or three times within the week for the strengthening and building of the system. It was directed that there be taken the beef juices for the purification of the blood; in this system, we find that this has not been prepared; these instructions have not been followed.

Now in giving instructions concerning healing or any of those other services that you would provide for the brethren, we would take the teachings of the Master in this manner. He often said, "Look about you and see what the world would do for a neighbor. Even he who is not the servant of God and is not called of God, will he not, when one is down, pick up his burden and help a neighbor, if that neighbor has been kind to him? It is only the enemy that the one of the world would fail to help." Then how would you call yourselves children of God if you would do only the same or even less than these children of the world? Then what would you do?

Then if you would be the healer, you must begin where the world begins that you would lift the burden of the one who is down and take that responsibility for his care. Doing then, those things that the world would do, so you have begun. Then being the child of God, you would go the second mile. Then where is the second mile? Even so when you pray each day during the morning hour, do you not say the words, "As I have health, so I give unto thee," and how would you give of your health to another? Would you not use your health in service to that one? Is this not then of the health to another? Then understand those teachings of your Master. Be what He would teach you to be. In such ways will healing then begin.

In one way further, you misunderstand the application of those laws of healing. Then see them given then in this manner, as was given earlier this day mind can be transmuted from plane to plane, from substance to substance, from quality to quality. Yet never frc n the lower to the higher, but always coming from the higher does it manifest in the lower, or see in this manner:

That all that is, is but a thought of God or seeing even further, that all that might be manifest would begin at a central point at an intensity of vibration that would produce no visible effect, nor an effect that could be sensed by any of your instruments, nor could it be measured nor seen nor weighed nor detected in any manner, for so fine would be the vibrations.

Then further and further, from the heart, from the mind of God; traveling further from the central purpose would the vibration become slower; would the substance then be of that vibration, that quality, [that would] become denser, more apparent. Then ranging further and further from Spirit, or from the finest, or that which is God, would you find that which is denser—or your plane. In such a manner might you understand that which is material.

Then if you would heal the material, would you take the hand to place on another's brow, that you might heal the other by transferring physical substance? Or would you see in this manner—but we find so many on this plane in the attempts to heal, who sit and feel such futile attempt at placing the hands here or there and expecting some physical feeling or transaction to take place, dealing then physically with the physical and attempting to transmute that which is on physical level. But then if you would heal even on a physical level, would you not forget that illness, and would you not do all in love that might be done to help the brother?

Then, might you busy yourself by lifting the spirits, creating a new atmosphere, lifting the vibration of all that is about, making all things cheerful, making all things bright; showing that I would care by preparing a meal and placing the vibrations. And if I would introduce physical vibrations into the body of another, then I would take the vibrations of my happiness or my physical body and place it into a meal prepared by my hands and so introduce my physical vibrations into the body of another that I would seek to heal.

Then mentally if you would deal with the person that is ill, cleanse the thought and prepare the mind and see that end result that you would expect to accumulate. Look at that which you would create and prepare it in the mind. Then use the mental body, use the mental forces [to create] that which you would have come into being ... holding then steadfastly to the truth hat which you would seek to create. As a creative being then, put this forth.

Then having done these, having created physically the atmosphere, and mentally created that which you would achieve, then would you sit and putting all aside, you would join the soul of him who lies upon the couch, and cause the spirits to take flight, leaving the physical plane then. Flying then on up, letting the self be released from these cares, from these denser planes, traveling closer to the heart of God, where the vibrations are higher, where there is not the density, where there is the origin of all thought, and where the two become one and here smiling and joyous would you lift the spirit in singing, in prayer, in worship, in laughter, and seeing the spirit healed, then would not the spirit then settle into matter, bringing such healing vibrations back into matter that nothing that is material could fail to respond?

But observe that which has been taught, and let him who would have no more than fifteen minutes or an hour be on his way, for often these things may take two hours a day. They may take seven days, but what man among you, if it be his child, his wife, his own body, would be the more concerned that it would be seven days than it be one day? Even so, care for thy brother as thyself, and learn the first law of God.

Now my brethren, until you learn these things and until you understand just how surely these things are given, thou shall not be able to apply those laws of healing. Until you are able to give all to strengthen a brother who is weak, thou canst not understand even the beginning of His laws.

Now, it has been given to you that even the Master Himself sat while learning and for hours mopped the fevered brow. He spent the time manipulating the diseased limbs with patience. He carried the water. He bathed the bodies. He cheered the spirit by singing. He played upon the harp.

Now brethren, there were the times when there would be spent the many hours of the day using the different methods of healing. Those might be seen to you as entertainment: the singing, the strumming of the harp, the telling of the stories-those methods calculated to change the mood, to lift the spirit. There were the times of fervent prayer for the lifting of the spirit. There were the times of bathing the body in the cool water for comforting. There were the times of the stimulating of the circulation by rubbing the hands and the feet. There were the assurances of love in the message in carrying out those unpleasant tasks. There were the telling of the anecdotes, the short stories to make one laugh. There were the painting of scenes, the pictures, the colors that were brought to surround the ones; yea, He studied all the laws of healing.

Understand this brethren for so must you do. For there is the need in this day that there would be those that would love: iso much] that they would give all, even in these ways, that those who suffer might be relieved. Then for what purpose would the spiritual servant be needed then to serve the sick? Why then would not the time be better spent on those sick in spirit, those who need the words of God? But brethren, understand, we would teach you love, for how could he go forth without love, teaching of Him who is love? But we would teach you love by making those sick among you—that you may so give of your health, one to another, thus learning the laws of love.

Then see those reasons for the illness among you and learn therefrom and give thanks. Laugh, be happy, be glad for such opportunity for service, for never have there been men so blessed as you who come in these last days to learn these last few lessons that would transmute those physical vehicles you inhabit into vessels fit for the chilren of the King. For in so changing these vessels, these vehicles, by blessing them with so much love, even the vibrations of thine own body will be changed to so much finer, higher rates of vibration, that these physical bodies will become light bodies and they will become not akin to that which is the physical earth, that which is material. And as the heaven and earth shall pass away and all shall be made new, so shall you be in that body that would be a part of the new and carrying His likeness into the higher manifestation of all that is.

Now understand children that which is brought and the reason that it is brought. So much have we given, so much has been recorded here, but so few have heard. What will you do with the words of the Master? We are through for now.

6002-6 (3-28-73)

EXCERPT 25

For in the developing of these hands, these fingers, can healing be transmitted from this body to others, so as well can teaching be given. This one could even communicate well with the minds of children not able to communicate in normal manners, or those retarded, those deaf and those blind could receive the vibrations, could receive knowledge from these hands. For there is such a level of sensitivity that could be given, or could be channeled in these manners.

Now understand, in the working of children it is not so much what is said, not so much what is done, but the thinking, that which thou are, that impresses children. For in these times, even as is taught in those classes conducted in this place, children of this age are receptive. Those minds that are becoming adjusted to operating through the human brain [are] still, we find, on the borders of the veil, or operating on both sides, both within and without the body, and are receiving programs from all levels of thinking and vibration.

So it might be described that these little ones are psychic and some never completely make that transition from other planes into the physical body, and are considered retarded. Yet if you would know the vibration of the soul, of the mind itself, these may be brilliant. These may be masters, only operating from outside the physical vehicle; and such are placed here that you might love, that you might express love upon a being incapable, apparently, of returning that love. And such would be the ultimate challenge for developing love and would you pray on this plane for an opportunity to develop love in the ultimate? So you would ask that one be placed before you, a Mongoloid, a retarded child, one not capable of returning your love. In such a manner would you be given that challenge, that opportunity to develop the ability to love as He loves.

So begin then now, and if you would teach, teach love, project love and be aware of that responsibility for that which occurs in the body of another when your hands are placed upon him. For even without your knowing or without his awareness, may your thoughts, your attitudes, your feelings be transferred into the body of another. And so may his vibrations, his auric field be altered, be changed by that which you are, that which you think. How often have these sources warned that you be careful what you think in the presence of one who is ill, or one with whom you would counsel, one who needs help.

Then in such a manner as you would enter a place to massage this one or that one, look upon the hands. See them as instruments of God, and always dedicate the hands to His purpose before touching another. Be aware of that responsibility that you take in manipulating the body of another human being, for he will not be left without your impression. Be aware of that which you set in motion upon touching any other human being on your plane, and [it would be] well that all should so dedicate themselves daily that [with] each person that I touch in this time and in this day if I shake a hand, if I hug another I am responsible for that which I do to his vibration, to his feeling. Therefore I dedicate myself at the beginning of this day to portray God and His presence to all with whom I come in contact. So might you give yourself to the developing of His vibration on this plane. It is in this manner, children, that you will prepare for His coming and make straight His paths that He may appear in the clouds.

1040 (4-13-73)

EXCERPT 26

We would find, then, concerning the relationships with those, particularly those in this Fellowship, and that one as has been questioned: We would find the relationship with_____in the Greek incarnation, when this one was a student of the drama. This is the incarnation that particularly affects the lifetime presently, and development — particularly in this manner—that this talent has been brought forward to be developed in this lifetime, and the life work for this one will be the studying and the teaching of drama. The attempts at professional acting, or, the times or development as an entertainer will fail as a profession, for this one should be teaching. The particular talents lie in the development of talents within others, the counseling, the coaching. This one, then, would be particularly gifted as a comedienne, and would play well those roles that would stimulate laughter in others. And realize that this is divine mission:

the lifting of spirits of others. Realize that through bringing the smiles, the laughter, to the face of those on this plane, you are responsible for counteracting a great deal of the anger, the hate, on this plane, and only by so doing, can this be counteracted; i. e., as these are produced—those vibrations of hate and anger—those that tear down the vibrations of this earth sphere. Then if there were so many more like this one, who could bring a smile to the lips, and joy to the heart, would you not lift the very vibrations of this planet by producing laughter, by producing enjoyment in the hearts of others? There is no greater service on this plane than that of entertaining in such manners as would produce smiles and laughter, would cause people to join together in love, for where is there room for hatred or animosity in a group of people laughing together? Do not their vi brations, even, join one with the other, and do they not become one in

that moment that they all become attuned to a particular "line" that produced the emotional reaction within that caused them to laugh together? Would this not, then, be a spiritual ministry of the highest order? See it in this manner, and train so many others to go out into the world, teaching people to laugh, to smile. Be this the ministry of this one.

6005 (12-16-72)

EXCERPT 27

Yes, we have this one, and these who have gathered here, and it is with pleasure that those are gathered here to look upon those instructions as would be channeled this day, and those memories that would come, for this one was Yilenas, who was with these who have gathered here in those times in Egypt when there were the services in the Temple called Beautiful and the Temple of Sacrifice. And there

were a number of those who have come and gathered in this place in this day who were of service in that day, and attempt, even in these latter days, to perfect those instruments of service as were used at that time.

We find then this artist, expressed as Yilenas, in that day when there was the use of art in the Temple Beautiful for the perfecting of the body and the mind, or that perfect balance of health, of creativities, that which would perfect the human vehicle, or the vessel, that would be used for the expression of God in the earth.

And it is because of this incarnation and the disciplines of that lifetime that there would be confusion in the art work in this day, for there would be within the memory the attempts to recall that which was done in that period, and the natural longing, the natural feeling in development would be to re-express that which was expressed in that day.

There are as well, however, those indications in the growth experience, the creative process, that would teach this one that there need be further development in this day, or different types of patterns, different expressions, than were used as were taught in the Temple Beautiful in that day. For those were expressed in this manner in that time: That as these came into the Temple of Sacrifice, where there were the services, as surgery, as medicine, as application of heat and light and electricity, the application of these devices that would be as medical or chemical, or of the types of adding to or taking away from the body—of physical means-here then were diagnoses made, and methods of treatment then were set. And those that might be given in the physical manner, or of the programming of the mind, or that as might be called hospital work, you see, was done here, then, in the Temple of Sacrifice.

These, then—these bodies that would be perfected then for theservice of God, or that would be further perfected as the human vehicle, were taken then to the Temple Beautiful, where here there were applied those arts, as music, as light, as color, as drama— these as affect the emotional, the spiritual, the creative expression of man—for the further perfecting of these bodies: Not that there would be the surgery or those disciplines of hospital use, you see, for this was, then, the more temple or the more worshipful, although those healing arts in that time, in that day, were seen as part of worship, so that Temple of Sacrifice in itself was a holy place. And never was there an instrument—the surgical instruments, or those that would be used in any way to touch the human body—that were not dedicated and attuned to the Divine, and for His purpose, so that all those who were the healers in that day were the priests, were the servants of God, and were required, even of those who would come before them, to be divinely attuned.

Would you not learn from that in this day, and see that one who would practice the medicine upon your body be attuned—an instrument of His service—and be a minister of the Divine, so that you would see your body as a temple of the Holy Spirit? Now see this in every detail of life, that you would treat this body as His holy temple, as a holy instrument. And it is not that you would gather in this place on one day a week that you would worship, but this worship is to take place in this temple during the week in all things that you do, and all contacts with your fellow man.

So there are great lessons that would come here for all who are gathered here, particularly for this artist, that there would be the recall of this lifetime and the purposes thereof. For as these were imperfect and had the imperfections in the body, that which needs to be cared for, that which needs to be stimulated, whether this would be a gland center or a thought within the mind or that which should be brought within the auric field—these were presented, then, before this artist, whose skillful eyes, then, and dedicated mind, the heart that sought to be of service (For this one was a priest in that day, and was male as might be expressed here, and would look about the aura of this one, and seeing about the body this or that, that was not brought into balance, or was of a color that should be corrected, or should be brought into balance through application of another color) then, could apply the healing lights, or the fields of color, the paints about the body, so that even these disciplines were brought onto the surface of the body.

Now, would you be aware in this day that so much that was created in that time, in that day, is being brought into the subconscious, the unconscious mind, of those in your world in this day, and would it seem strange that these things are manifesting on this plane in this day in such other forms as are not dedicated to His service? For you find in this day such application of ultraviolet light, and would this not come to the unconscious mind, the subconscious mind, these who would sit under such colors, opening then the chakras through mechanical means, or introducing the chemicals into the body, leaving self open, then, to those lower than incarnate spirits, or those discarnates, those lower elements of earth, those that would seek to manifest through human bodies, or the discarnate spirits? Or that which might possess the human body would be so attracted around these who would open self and would leave the body to travel, and to be in other planes.

And these disciplines that have come, or these pleasurable activities, as these ones would seek, giving up responsibilities for the body, then, leaving them open to such possession, would you not see as indication of the subconscious, or the teaching from even this day when there was the learning of the laws of God; that these have be- come inclined, then, at these times to use that which you have called the black light, or the ultraviolet ray, or these force fields of radi ation, then that would protect the body according to the laws of the universe? Then would not the Heavenly Father look after thee, even in thy times of foolishness?

See, then, that these periods of recall, these disciplines learned so early upon the earth, are not lost, but come into the discipline, into the life, come to the surface as they are needed. And as you would see these things and bring them to the surface, and cause them to manifest, so shall ye be able to perfect these bodies, these vehicles, these vessels, that have been given for the expression of the Divine.

See then and in this time the application of one another in those disciplines of massage, in the body painting, in those giving of self to one another in these manners that have come not as the expression, not in the services as in that day, not in the Temple of Sacrifice or the Temple Beautiful, or that which you have called the church, but of the giving individually of self to self. Would this not, then, if the mind were pure and the heart clear and clean—would this not, then, be worship? As the one would paint upon the other body, would not the vibrations be lifted, attuned and healed? If these purposes were pure, then, and given in a worshipful manner, would not healing be introduced? Now, see that which surrounds the body in color and light, and train the eye to be aware of that which comes in, and in so becoming aware, would you not introduce about the body the light waves of the other lengths, or that that would rectify those colors that you would see out of balance?

3016 (2-25-73)

EXCERPT 28

We would see the many talents brought over from past lifetimes, particularly that this one was a harpist in the Temple Beautiful, and used the music of the harp for the healing of the physical body. And this can be seen at this time in the mind, and as there is the relating to the music of the harp, this one can see the particular body areas that would be affected by the plucking of certain strings. See these tones within the mind, hear them within self, and see those problems as would be healed in others, particularly in the limbs: the twisted or withered limbs are particularly responsive to certain levels of vibrations, rhythms of music, particularly the harp music. For there were those creatures at this time who were not quite human, or that is, they were being transmuted from animal bodies to those bodies that would be perfected for the human race, and there was treatment in the Temple Beautiful for these bodies by the use of music. Attempt to see this with the mind's eye and realize that by producing this music within the heart, or deep within self in meditation and prayer, ... at the same time as this is being produced within self, there can be projected healing power toward those who would need the type of vibration. Attempt to attune self to this type of music and realize that music has color. All these are different manifestations of light along a spectrum and attempt to see color and rhythm and music integrated into one. Realize that life itself is but a vibration, a rhythm, and as these are attuned they become one, and all things that have rhythm or vibration have healing potential.

Bring these then as a part of life and integrate life. There are those who suffer on this plane for no other purpose than to be an opportunity to demonstrate the perfect laws of healing. They are ill on this plane that we might discover the means, the methods of healing, of correcting these problems, and in so doing learn the principles, the applications of the laws of the universe. And in discovering these vibrational qualities in music, in art, in beauty, in color, in nature—in believing in these as the perfect laws of God— we discover His laws and come closer to God and lift the entire race a little closer to the Godhead.

4004 (10-23-72)

EXCERPT 29

Particularly for this one the expression would come in drawing that which would come as thought impressions or energy impressions, vibrational fields or force fields of energy and vibration that would come as impressions in the mind. These would be given as line drawings in colored pencil. They will come as inspiration from the mind but for the present they will take the form of geometric shapes one within the other. Expressing that which I would see as the color of anger, the color of hate, the color of love, expressing these together as the interplay would come — as the interplay between vibrations.

These then would be abstract drawings going from one color into the other. There would be the imaginative ideas of what would happen if this force field or this energy vibration would come into contact with this other manifestation or energy or level of vibration. In seeing this there will be created the feelings that could be demonstrated, that which takes place within the life force. There would be the studying of the aura as well, and in the realization of the manner of which these colors manifest, there could be drawn the energy vibrational fields.

Now this may be performed or may be understood or brought into being, better related for this one by drawing a tiny cross in black on the forehead of another person. Sitting against a neutral colored wall, and at a distance of some ten feet, there would be the concentration on the tiny cross and the relaxation, careful not to look at that which would manifest as the aura and as there is the practice of this after several days there will the manifestation of color. Now be not satisfied when these manifestations of color come for they will be-come more and more advanced until there will be the ability to see the lack of attunement in one manner or another. That is, disease or injury will show up in the body as manifestions in this color field...

4003 (10-19-72)

EXCERPT 30

This one learned the medical conditions or the healing methods through the healing of plants; and through studying of the growth of plants and through the protection of same, this one learned the application of the laws of healing to the human body as well. It would be then through the studies, through the growth of plants and the comparison of that which happens when these are loved or hated, through the application of music and color around plants. Study the effect of the painted wall around a plant of particular colors. Move these to different positions, bring interplay around the plants, these different colors that would affect their growth and see that which happens, that which stimulates and that which would retard the growth, the development, and understand as well that which occurs in the human in relation to color, music, the vibration of love.

In so understanding and applying that which would come naturally, that which one would be drawn to, so will you understand that which is the talent and that which is the life work. And if you would understand the life work, see that to which you are drawn naturally, and that which would respond to thy touch. This then is that which you have developed and can be used in His service.

6004-2 (5-30-73)

Music & Art

Now to that that has been the question of the soul, of the heart. In developing the expression, particularly through music, through those combinations of words, we would find in this way. There is given here, a specific talent, and there are those on inner planes as we would find – or for the purpose of description, we would say that on the inner plane would all or a complete portion of music or piece or manuscript be set together as a pattern, and before being channeled to this plane or before being available to the composer or that one that would set upon paper, or express, would be complete there.

Then there are those who see those patterns of music as being expression of the Divine, that seek then, contact with those souls by pouring forth into their consciousness the music or the inspiration through this. Then understand at those times when there would come an urge, when there comes music or patterns of music that would seem to flow, that these are times of contact or the attempts to open a door – those attempts to pull aside the veil.

Now at those times, set thee down and pour out that which is in the heart; yet, afterward then, sitting, sitting quietly, for in these times will greater realizations come, not in words, not in that that may be spoken, but in those words beyond words, for these are the kinds of growth. Then as you would raise the self up then, to go about the daily task, you would find that the knowledge, the wisdom, is greater, is deeper, not for that teaching that has come in words or patterns of symbols as you would find in your language, but for the opening up of that remembrance of the Divine from within or that that might be expressed as soul development. These would come in these times.

Then if there be the writing, the setting down of these patterns of music and the bringing of words and these combinations, would these then necessarily express religious or spiritual concept. But we find thus, and understand for this one should study much the construction of music, for those patterns in music or those scales, those tones of the scale would relate to those chakras, those centers of the body. And the vibration of the particular chakra then, would vibrate or open or stimulate – cause growth within those body centers so that as there is played the specific patterns of music, this or that different type, as these then would play upon the emotions, they as well would affect through their specific level of vibration that vibration of the chakra or the life center of the body corresponding then to these vibrations of course, or combinations of vibrations, so that there is produced a pattern that can be for the growth or for the detriment.

Then understand that music can awaken within the soul the wild beast or the gates of hell, as might be described, or could soothe, could calm the beast and awaken the God within. Then see that it is for the purpose and find that that is aroused, not by the words set to the music, but by the music. Feel that, analyze that inside, that is aroused by the strain or the movement of the music and see then whom it would serve.

Now not in the combinations of words set in such a pattern as to teach, or that is, not that the lyrics would be expressive of a religious thought, though this be well at times that it be so, yet see that you would be of service in putting together that which only would seem to be entertaining on the surface. Yet there would be in those combinations of words, those words would be found pleasing and calming, building, though not expressing necessarily a concept of religion, of spirit, of thought; yet at the same time set with that music that would cause the building of the soul, the attuning of those body centers to central purpose – so even would you produce healing in the physical body – at the same time raising the level of awareness. And this be thy ministry. Now study that it be so.

For there is given here specific talent and can be directed for these purposes and feel within thine own body as there is the setting apart of music and creating these tones and these movements, feel those body centers, those chakras, and see how these be affected in the various ways with the combinations of music. Play the many different types then and feel those ways in which thine own body is stimulated and sitting in meditation, hear that music beyond the music or the music of the spheres, for there is the ability within this one to tune the self, to tune the hearing to such fine point in those times of meditation, or the bringing of stillness within the physical body, that you could tune the self to that which is put forth as music.

Then going beyond those constructions of music you would go beyond the ability to hear on the physical plane, and go to that inner level so that there would be the bringing to a fine attunement, (there are no words to express that which would occur here) for you would go beyond music as you see it constructed on your plane and hear then the music of the spheres. And in so attuning would you find the nature of that inner peace and manner in which it would affect the body, the gland centers. And in such a way would you perfect the ability to heal the physical body through those strains of music – through attunement.

Now understand children, as there is given those stories that have been passed from generation to generation, these have been inspired even though coming from those commonest of folks as you might refer, and imaginative tales as they have been seen and we refer in this moment to that tale of the Pied Piper, for there was great teaching that was attempted to be channeled through from inner planes in the giving of such a fanciful tale. Then understand that power that is in music, for in this day much destruction has come from those patterns that have come. Those patterns of music in recent times have been the expression of fear, of hate, of disturbance in the heart of those young, poured out over the airwaves, and these surrounding the earth then with expressions of souls crying out, moaning in pain. And there come in these times the many who at-tempt to bring music into such control, such patterns as would lift consciousness, would lift the vibrations of this planet a little closer to God. And know that those given such abilities for putting together those strains of music even could lift the vibrations of these planets so that they would ease that travail, those birth pains, that come upon this planet as He would give birth to those higher levels of all that is manifest.

Then see no greater ministry than the ability to lift the heart, to lift the consciousness of these, to attune these to the strains of music and be about that business, not necessarily that words would be set in a way to express concepts of God or of the Divine, yet concepts of peace, concepts of nostalgia as it were, or the awakening of those things that are beautiful within the heart, the expressions of beauty, of peace, of love.

Know that it is not the man who would put together the words of the great sermon, but him who could affect the heart in love, or produce an effect in another man that would cause him to express God. Understand these concepts, children, and see it in the mind's eye. In this moment would you see a man standing facing another man and with his smile, with the love that he pours out, causes the other to smile. Now has he not caused that man in that moment to express God? See how simply you may serve?

It is not through the great deeds that attract attention and cause great movements among men, but it is the face to face, person to person act that would bring joy, that would bring the expression of God, whether it be beauty or a humming strain – humming under the breath – and in such ways men are attuned. And as you would go about the business daily, it might be well for all that there would be the humming under the breath, constantly attune, that would lift the soul running through the mind. In such ways would you attune to the Divine. For such lifting music is divine and is of the nature of God Himself. And in such ways you would constantly attune the self, then, to His presence.

8031 (7-23-73)

EXCERPT 32

[This entity was] given to the purposes of music in the temple or the call to worship as would be spoken, and that instrument [in use] was, as might be described, a type of harp, though on a frame much larger than you would find in existence or even know at this time. And it had the ability to be heard for large areas, or it expanded itself, or set in motion vibrations that carried for some two to three miles. Yet [these vibrations were] not in an offensive [form], even in proximity, for these vibrations moved the stillness of the air for large periods; and they depended not on the setting in motion of a large volume of noise or sound at the location of the instrument, but reacted, as were as might be described, at a distance.

Now there could be discovered, and will in this time in some few years in this period, be discovered those methods of projecting sound in such ways, or bouncing sound against those movements that exist in the atmosphere, or those waves, those circles about same as these are set in motion. So, that sound is created at a distance and brought toward the instrument rather than sent out from it.

We find, then, the use of the music to assist in the ability to drop those [undesirable bodily] appendages, or correct that [formation] of the bodies. And those temples that were set up for the worship there and those temples set up or created for sacrifice were for the giving of the bodies, that there would be the returning in those corrected or improved bodies. And if you would understand those systems that were set in operation there, they would not be seen as so cruel or in-human as are now thought of in those systems of human sacrifice set up even by this series or strain of priests as entered there...

[Now] those on this plane in this time [today] seek to develop that of music that would be as compared with the cooking or the taking into the system of food highly seasoned and [with] ... much pepper used. Now see that these affect the body or the emotions of the soul in the same manner. For pepper is an irritant to the system and is taken for such purpose that would tickle, would stimulate.

So in the music in this time are there brought those discordants, that which would be displeasing, inharmonious and would be exciting to the system as the abrasiveness in the sexual nature. And so then those chakras rather than developing or opening as a flower bud, would be yanked or forced open, thus setting the flower into intense vibration or shock or nervousness. So that found in the opening of the chakras would be distorted, and these... [having]

opened them in such manners, whether by drugs or by the intensity of such music as has been brought so popular in this time, would find that which they think of as the God concept, yet it would be so shattering, so nervous a concept, that [it would] distort the image or the face of the Father or God. So then these chakras are damaged. So is the ability to think or to understand, to reason damaged, and so that all the love nature becomes distorted then and expresses the baser natures of love and not that of growth.

Now if you would understand music, understand in these manners: That this ... can be used for soul development if there be used the harmonious, [or this] ... can be used for the destruction of the soul of the universe if used in the discordant or in destructive manners.

Now, that difference in the black and white magic, that difference in the left hand and right hand path, that difference in good and evil, are the manner in which those same laws are applied. There is one law. That applied for self or for destruction becomes evil. That same law applied for the building, for harmony, becomes good. Understand then that music is the tool. Developing and dedicating to the purposes of the Father can lead those of this plane straight to the throne of God and can heal the body, can attune the heart.

There is no limit to that that might be accomplished in the treatment of the mentally ill through the application of those proper harmonious tones of music applied for the soothing, applied for the stimulating of the proper areas, the proper glands. So many among these find chemical imbalances within the body for the disproportionate manufacturing or secretion of the glands. Through the balance of music then, . . . that taken into the system could be rebalanced and could be found to function more productively, as a result of that one expressing himself or attuning himself to the instrument and pouring that of his love, or that of the higher nature, or that of God through the strains of music for purposes of healing.

Then in that question you would ask then, there have been given many here of the higher aspects or purposes of music. What then will you do with same? How would you develop? Would you have us give here those manners, those methods for the developing of same or would you take that which we have offered as possibility and find, discover, develop within the self? For the talents are here. The intelligence is given. All opportunities lie [open]. Then lift same and apply for a purpose.

If we would give here all that might be needed for the development, for the understanding, or if we would reveal all those laws governing same, well it might be for our spiritual growth on this plane. But what would be accomplished in thine? Take that we have offered and make it the steps of a ladder that might lead to a proper use of those tones of that sacred scale given of God for application.

8030 (8-11-7)

EXCERPT 33

Then, consider within self that [response] produced through music, or the manners in which the levels of the system, the emotions, and that of the body or the physical changes within the body are conducted by music. For it will be found that particular glands respond to particular chords – or, that is, this could be described as the pituitary attuned to the key of C, and that of the thymus attuned to E natural, [and] that of the reproductive to the key of A.

And those [affinities] should be discovered, or added, or developed through the study of one given to such; or, that is, that you would research within the body, and striking those chords, measure the responses of the glands.

Then [study] these [chords] relating to the chakras, and see that that would cause the development or the opening of the chakras in relation to a particular key, or chord, or note, or vibration or rhythm. For it would be found that all in this universe are attuned to particular rhythms. And expanding beyond that concept of music, find that study as has been referred [to] as biorhythm or those natural rhythms of the human body.

All these as studied and correlated one to the other would ...

[demonstrate] that the entire system or universe is attuned to music, or, that is, music in its broadest sense as rhythm. So, understanding these you would begin to have greater respect for that rhythm in the life; or, that is, rising daily at the same time, retiring nightly at a particular time, setting the periods for the meals at a particular time, and worshiping, meditating at the same given time daily.

So, you would find that you would set in motion the body attuned to itself, the soul then attuned to the body and the mind – these working in harmony or striking a chord that would be in harmony one with the other.

So would such a man, even one never studying those concepts of God, or that which you have thought of as spiritual growth – such a man simply becoming at harmony with himself would discover that God concept within himself and would become attuned to the procession of this universe, and attuned to the spirit, the activity, the nature of God. So, then would he become God in the activity, ascending then to the Father or becoming one with that which is the operation of the universe.

Now in this manner did Pythagoras set in motion those descriptions of the spiritual laws according to the attunement of music or mathematics, or that beginning of that now known as physics. There is not a study that you might find upon this plane of any form of natural science that would not eventually lead the man, in its highest development, to the nature of God

Now we would suggest that this one would make available to self those testing machines or apparatus that would show the difference in the responses of this human body, or . . . [use] the polygraph, the galvanic skin response tester, the brainwave machine, in some manner as would test the level of brain wave activity. Through the studying upon one's self and others of the effects of music, so will these be understood. There are those who will assist in such research if these are sought out in this particular field.

Give assistance with this one, where there is opportunity and continue such research, learn the laws of healing through music, for so will you discover so many things that will be invaluable....

Know that [there is] spiritual music, or that music can be a spiritual tool, a tool for spiritual therapy as well as physical therapy. Know that messages from the planes of. ... those higher levels, from those higher spheres, can be translated, can be revealed, can be brought through music. Understand that spirits can be lifted and caused to soar.

We will see that there are physiological changes that take place in the body, as the mind, as the emotions are stirred through application of music, [through] both its rhythms and tones. Understand that the body vibrates according to rhythm. There is, in music, all that is needed to heal any human body, to cause these bodies to heal themselves by the correct application of those chemical contents of the atmosphere, by the changing of electrical vibration. Know that even adjustments ... [may] be made in the spine, in the vertebrae, by the application of the vibration of music – that such healing applied in such manners as can be discovered and applied by this one. So those muscles which tense, which pull one vertebra from the other, and cause those subluxations in the spine, and the uneven flow, the lack of a healing flow, from the lines from the intelligence of the brain to those portions of the body as are needed – these could be corrected by the relaxing and the stimulating influences of music, bringing balance in the human body

7025 (4-30-73)

EXCERPT 34

For [this artist] then, we would see the Soul Pattern in this manner: That the Soul Pattern as put on paper would be, rather than the perfection of the individual, would show forth that which has already come into the life, or that which has been done with past lives. So then, in the Soul Pattern type of drawing as would be introduced through this one, or would be channeled to the paper, would be seen on the lower portions thereof, that which was done in the early incarnations in this Earth. And there might be seen in that oldest soul   those periods of light entering through the bottom, as there was the creation of the light: the sun, the moon, the stars, [that it] might come in through those portions. Then those early lives of such perfection on earth. Then, above these, might come that chaos that developed in such as the fall, and then those lifetimes that were used for the further development.

Then, these Soul Patterns, that which will be called the Soul Pattern, will be seen as drawings that would express that which has been done with opportunity. In the upper portions, then, might be given that which comes in the future as opportunity for development, then, following the individual [through] that which has been done, those lessons that come in, and these indications of opportunity for the future. So that the Soul Pattern as given would be the three-fold drawing, then, and might be compared to the Archetype. Then one who has received such archetypical drawing, or the perfection in detail and in color that should be brought into the life, would compare this, then, with the Soul Pattern. Or, this drawing concerning that that has been the part of the akashic record, or the revelation of that record that would be carried thereabout, or the drawing of the aura and all that would be surrounding this-as has been called by the [Edgar] Cayce source, the Auric Pattern or the Auric Drawing [Aura Chart] – would be the Soul Pattern, as it has been called then by this artist. And there would be seen that which has been done with past lives, that which has been built, bringing the opportunity then. See as opportunity, [for] all that has been built in past lives comes in the present as opportunity, or tools that build for the present, for the future.

See the center then, as those accumulated tools, and the upper portions thereof of such a drawing as being the application of these tools, or those opportunities for the application of the past life, for the perfection, for that that might be done in this lifetime. So, using this three-fold drawing to unfold that which would be the purpose of this life, so can these drawings be of service in such ways.

Now, as instruction for the development of drawings of this type, we would give in these manners: that there would be the contemplation by this, the artist, the dedication of self at the beginning of such periods, for the purpose, the contemplation of that person who comes and his need, and sensing, feeling, being aware of his need. Then you would proceed with that as you have called the Divine Plan or that might be given as the archetypical drawing, not that the Divine Plan drawing and the archetypical drawing necessarily be the same; but this third type, the Divine Plan, would combine those of the archetype with the Soul Pattern – that which has been done, that which may be done, with the Archetype, which would be perfection, or the ending pattern, that which would be sought to be brought in. With the third impressing, then, the Soul Pattern with the Archetype, would come that perfection, bringing in what have I done in past lives with the tools in this time – that which I may do. I would combine with the Archetype, or that which should have been, producing a third: that which may come now. Or the Pattern, that which God would have me produce, would be the third, or the Divine Plan type of drawing, showing what I will attempt to bring in this life, or that which is possible, that which the Lord has set apart for me.

Now for those that would come and would hear these words, these lips that would speak, see in this manner: not only on paper, but also in those processes of daily life, may you find all these three types. There is naught expressed on paper, or in art, or in the music, that could not be brought as well from those vibrations of daily life, or the intercourse between individuals, that you might not see. As you would see perfection in the landscape, in the universe, would this not be the archetypical drawing that might be brought to your attention even by the sunset? And this is what I would seek to express, and I see the colors of the sunset and their beauty; and God, may I take into myself and into my system such color that I may show forth Thy glory. May I express Thy glory in this world!

So might you pray in seeing the colors, the perfection, the Archetype, that which God has set apart that you would be. As the heavens express His handiwork, so might those beings on earth give self for His expression in this way. Then, as this one humbly would attempt to put these expressions of the universe on the paper that these might be inspired to service, use this in daily life. Then the Soul Pattern:

Look upon yourself and that which you have created. See the

talents that you have brought into this lifetime Soul Pattern, even that might be put on paper. What have you been given? What body has been given? The body that you have been given is exactly what is needed for the service at this time. If this body be obese or underdeveloped, would it not be for the purpose that you might perfect this for the glorification of God? It is not given by accident, but that which you have created, that which you have brought in is for the perfection of God. And would you see the one in the perfect body as expressing God more perfectly than others? We would say no, but only in the perfection of the body, only in the taking of that raw material and bringing it into perfection is God expressed. Then what will you do   with what He has given? This then would be the Soul Pattern: All that you are, you have created. This you have brought into this world for the perfection of God, and there is not the possibility for one that is not given to the other, that all could not express the perfection of God, even the Christ force!

Now pray for the body through which we speak. Pray that these vibrations might be held in check that we might continue that which has been brought, for there is much gathered here that would be channeled to all in this time. Bring healing, then, into your own body, into your own mind. Open the ears that you may hear, for there is much that will come.

Now my children, know My voice. And you who would walk, even in the garden with Me, give of yourself for these purposes in this day. Understand that seventh day that is set apart. Come often in these ways, that you would share in the worship. Be blessed by the gathering in this way. By so blessing one another in love, you do show forth My presence in this world till the glory be seen in the clouds.

Now, we would seek that all would understand, and use those talents that are given, with those records that have been brought of this one, and such opportunity to show forth beauty in this world and to be of service. And even as there is the attempt here, with those of the masters who are gathered to give all that may be given for this individual, there is not the possibility that we could restrain that which should be given forth to the world. But we must go beyond this individual and these individual records, and speak to all who have gathered here, for the vibrations would not be held to a single record, the single individual. We can only take that that is brought of these records and raise to these higher levels that you may take and [use] that which is her single talent, and apply to your own life, that all may be of service in such manners.

Know, then, it is the manner in which these things are done that expresses His glory, and it is the wish in the heart in such creation that would apply for the perfection of self and others. So may this art, these colors, be used for healing in this day even as they were used then in this Temple called Beautiful. And, as they expressed miracles and changed human bodies from the animal form to the perfected form that man may walk upright, because of such application of color even on paper and in lights and in paints upon the body, so even in this day, if there would be the belief among those who would call themselves the children of Christ or the Little Christs in this world today – if you would but believe, there are not limits to that which might be created in this day, even as were given in that.

Now how could you doubt that He would walk with thee? Would He not even want that He might be expressed in your presence this day? Has He not promised that as you would gather in His name there He will sit in your midst? And how would you doubt that He has joined you even here in this moment in this room? Now, is there an act of healing that He cannot perform? Is there an act of perfection that He cannot give? Would He not express His being forth into this world if so allowed? Then, be the clay in the Potter's hands. Be molded, yield to His presence, and express that which He would be in this world.

Thou art the body of Christ. Then, if that muscle yield not to that which the brain would create or would have it do, would not the body be spastic, or even paralyzed, out of control? Ye are the body of Christ. Let His will, then, be that which would command thy movements, and cause this body to function together as a whole, each of you acting as a portion thereof. Be ye one in His name, that His work may be glorified, that His name may be spoken in your midst, and that men may know His good works through your coming together, and glorify the Father which is in Heaven. And if there be one among you in disharmony, or if there be a portion of thy body in disharmony, that which would be out of balance, then accept the Christ into that body, and allow that perfection to come of Him. Then look upon those drawings, those paintings that would be channeled through this one, and bring into self, accept into self, those colors that have been placed before you, then, that you might express His beauty, His love. See self reflected, and bring it forth into the world. Be ye perfect, even as your Father in Heaven in perfect. This came as His command.

Now, that there might be the greater use, then of this work, this ministry of this one, we would give these instructions: that you would see these different ministries on the paper, and give to these that which should be brought in the art field, that which would be worked upon. And those symbols of occupation, those symbols of development that would come in showing that work that was done in past lives might be indications of talent that this one might develop and bring forth in this life. That one who was unaware of his hidden inclination toward music might, then, give self to the development, and might receive guidance, counseling, through the paper if there be the symbols of the past incarnations, of the occupations there, that there might be the channeling, the development of perfection in this lifetime.

See, then, that these would be brought in: those memories of past incarnations, those colors that need to be developed within the body, those strengths, that which this one has brought into the lifetime to perfect. And, if these would be channeled, if this artist would bring these from past lives, might there not be the fear that is expressed, even at this moment, that I might not be able to bring these things: How will I understand? How will I bring these indications from past lives? How can I be so clear a channel?

And we would speak in this manner: This body has been given for a service. Such a great talent would not be given without the requirement of much in return. This body, then, is the temple of the Holy Spirit, and it would be given that you would give of your time each day, in a disciplined manner, that you might develop those understandings of Spirit, and channel those instructions of God that would come not only in the drawing and with the drawing, but might be spoken through the lips and through the heart the awareness, the counseling. That might be given with these drawings, with the color, that there might be the help in the developing of these.

3016 (2-25-73)

Reincarnation & Karma

EXCERPT 35

Conductor: Is reincarnation a truth? If so, why do a surprising number of spiritualists profess not to believe in it and why is there such confusion on this issue?

And now in giving such an answer, there are so many factors to be considered. Yet we would offer these. See that manner in which the Christ taught, the Master Himself, in this plane. He never gave emphasis to that of reincarnation, so this was done for a purpose. For rather than projecting the idea of incarnating again and again on this plane to accomplish a purpose, yet He pointed to that development that goes beyond the need for manifesting in the physical or the human body.

Then the teaching of these to prepare the self for a successive lifetime, or for another time in this plane then, would have pointed to something less than that ultimate development or to returning to the Father. Thus He spoke not of the intermediate stages or the many lifetimes that might be required for attaining such soul growth, but pointed directly toward that home of the soul or the returning to that Father Himself, thus giving no emphasis to reincarnation. For this only is a tool for such growth, for such steps toward the Father. So it is that His purpose, in not giving emphasis to such, exists.

Then as to those who are referred [to] as the spiritualists, see that which they worship. For what is their attention placed on? It would be placed not on returning to the Father or attaining those states of onemanship with God, or at-one-ment with the Father, or returning to that utmost expression of being again with Him. Yet would the consciousness be given only to communicating with those passed into the netherworld or the inter-between – that plane particularly of those souls caught not in higher development or seeking the Father, but rather hovering about and showing that interest in things of the flesh or things of this world and those who remain on this plane.

But seek to communicate with those whose attention or mind is pointed ever upward toward the Father. Yet these [will] be reluctant to communicate with those of Earth, for their interest is not upon the Earth or the things of the Earth. It would be understandable then that those who seek to keep spirits bound about the plane of the Earth, that there be the possibility of communicating, would not be willing to accept the idea that these go beyond and are offered the opportunity for coming again.

Would this then deny the possibility of communicating with such souls as left consciousness or left the physical some years hence, or centuries even? Not so, for understand that built on this plane is personality, is consciousness, is achievement, and these remain a part of the records. Then that which would be contacted by the spiritualist as that consciousness of the voice, that personality of the one who would be brought and manifested, exists in a very real way. Yet that soul is not bound thereto, for the personality was left on this plane as the soul went beyond. Then the soul went beyond. Then the soul has not been contacted. But that personality or that which is discarded, is earth bound, may yet be contacted even centuries hence.

Then one is not wrong and the other right. Yet there are levels of understanding. If there be the ability to understand these things, then there is not so much disagreement.

Conductor: Are we as souls free to choose the age in which we will come back, the time or period of history that we choose? Or can we sense the souls we will have future contact with, and does this Infinite Intelligence direct us?

That is so very difficult to explain in those words or the limitations of language, for we would say yes, that all would [choose] by their consciousness or by that which is attracted toward [them, or] that magnetism, or those laws of like attract like. In such a manner is each soul attracted to those conditions best for him. Yet it is as well true that infinite knowledge or the Father Himself would direct those possibilities and give guidance here, yet not superseding the will of that soul. For that soul is given much opportunity, yet not free reign, as to assuming this condition or this time and place.

But there are those as have been referred [to] as the Lords of Karma. Or that you might be better able to understand: There are those controls of conscience, or the higher self, that are as the nature or natures of God and so have contact with the angels themselves. So there is much opportunity for advice, for direction, for assistance, for help from those higher levels of consciousness. Yet there is free will or opportunity to enter those conditions that are best for each individual soul's development. Then [there is] not so much conscious choice as that which was built in life creating those conditions under which one must manifest.

Then that choice is made now on this plane. And what conditions would you enter in the next life that [are] chosen here and now? Upon what would you place your consciousness and what would you value? Those things will you be attracted to. And if they be those things of the flesh and if that of pain and corruption is sowed here, so will it manifest. As the tree falleth, so shall it lie. Or in such a manner shall the body be picked up again, in the manner that you laid it down.

Conductor: Do animal souls reincarnate?

Not as simply stated, yet they may, you understand, [in] that these [animals] are steps in the evolution of a consciousness. Or that is, that animals would not have individual consciousness as such, but would be vehicles, would be tools as a group for the developing of that which would become individual consciousness and would incarnate in the higher vessels or vehicles.

#4030 (7-24-73)

EXCERPT 36

Conductor: Please give me some guidance in helping me to understand the confusion surrounding my personal life in this time.

All the confusion we see as personal feelings of guilt. And [there is] misapplication of the term karma in this life, for there is felt within this one that such positions have been placed in life because I owed this one or that one a debt in some manner.

Understand, and this may be applied to any soul on your plane, you are not judged according to that which you owe to any particular soul, whoever he may be. All judgment is within the self. And that which you would meet on the plane would be the self. Nor would you owe any man any debt as long as you have forgiven any one who has erred. Then if anyone has hurt you, has caused you harm, and you have not yet forgiven him or her, then you have a debt to that person. If you have caused harm to another, you have no debt to him. The debt is only to yourself, that you would right the situation. And it need not be with that same one. It is only where there is lack of forgiveness to another that you would owe any debt.

Now understand karma in these ways. That which any soul would meet on this plane is owed only to self. Then those others that would be brought in to the lifetime for the payment of karmic debt are only brought for the convenience, in that this one or that one would be of the particular type or create the situation that would allow you to meet self.

Then understand you owe only to the self and thy God. Then look for that which would be the best use of the lifetime and the situations of the lifetime. And if you would understand, "What is right for me to do in my life at this time?" then step out of self, above the body, and look down upon those situations that face the self. Look dispassionately upon thyself and judge yourself accordingly, saying, "I am God, I am the Most High. And I look down upon those situations that have come into the life of my child Joan at this moment. And what would I expect that she should do with these situations that have come?" And so judging from above, know that you are one with the Father. And if you would not condemn the one, Joan, thy child, then would thy Father not forgive thee?

Now understand all condemnation is within the self. And as you would forgive, so would the Father forgive. And as you would condemn, so would the Father condemn. Then condemn not the self, but forgive. And build with that thou hast, that you may grow to use to best advantage that which has been given in this lifetime. And as you would find talent, so put them to use, that others may be helped. And do not cling to that which has been in the past, nor fear that you have hurt this one or that one, or owe a karmic debt here or there. If you would erase all karmic debt to all other living souls, then forgive everyone about. Then forgive the self and begin to build. Do not cling to debts, to fears, to lack. Where you have failed, there will be opportunity to build tomorrow. Then cling not to the failure, but look towards the lessons, the building that will come. Be about the Father's business, and all the confusion will fade.

#6004-2 (5-30-73)

EXCERPT 37

Conductor: You will give specific advice concerning the occurrence of the death of this one and the rebirth of this one within the same lifetime, as we know it. What was the direct change in this entity when this death occurred, and what were reasons behind this change? Also, did this change the spiritual awareness of this one, and how, and for what reasons?

Now we bring you greetings in His name, for thou art Estala, prophetess of the Essenes, and should remember those experiences of being among the guardian people as the Master walked upon the earth. We would find that this one has a great deal of knowledge within. But this would not mean that there is to be the teaching, the displaying of this knowledge, in this lifetime. For this one has returned in this final lifetime to perfect those laws of God. That is, to lift that one who is the soulmate and cause the realization in those about her of the very closeness of the Master Himself. For deep within the heart of this one could be the realization, the awareness, that she has touched the hand of Him who was the Christ. She has seen His face and spoken with Him. She has walked with Him in the still hours of the night, in the cool garden breezes, and would realize his teachings deep within the heart.

Though these may not be expressed on outer or surface levels, they are seen in the face, they are seen in the attitudes of others. Not that this one would be the example of perfection, but there is an innate awareness of that oneness of all creatures.

Now it would be given for this one that it would not be possible that such a one blessed by the Master Himself would not carry about self a vibrant radiance of His presence in this lifetime. For we would see that in the lifetime as Estala, there were the moments of astral projection, or that is, that this one had the ability and had been trained so that the body might manifest in two places simultaneously, that work might be carried out.

Now these things might be done for the good of those on your plane. That is, if there is the need to be at a distant place for the blessing or for the welfare of another individual, that this might be accomplished even in this lifetime. For we find that this is that which occurred in the instance, which is being spoken of. It is necessary that it occurred at that time, that there be the realization of self and of the purposes of this incarnation. It would be given that there was advanced spiritual awareness in that lifetime. It was not that this one was changed, or that another entity or spirit was added, or any of those things which have been the questionings. It was simply that this one stepped outside the body – much in the manner as does this trance source through which we speak – and looked down upon the body and saw it as it is seen from inner planes. That is, saw the worlds, saw the relationships between men in the manner in which it is seen from the inner planes, or the higher planes, as you will. It would be seen that when there is left behind the body of clay on your level, that the awareness of the soul would join those others on the inner plane where there are the Lords of Karma.

Now the Lords of Karma are given as a term that you may realize those laws or rules that you would apply in judging the lifetime, or that which is accomplished in an incarnation. Not that these are entities, but they would be seen by those on your planes as entities, for purposes of reference.

It would be seen then that this one voluntarily left the human body and came to join the Lords of Karma for the assessment of the incarnation and what should be done. For this one came not because there was the need for incarnation in this lifetime, but because there were the ones who would need the help. This one came on a mission then, to be the catalyst to bring others closer to the Godhead.

It is not meant that this one be the evangelist or the great healer. It is meant, however, that this one realize the potential of such existence. That is, one who would carry in self the very Christ force, all of the vibrations of the Christ Himself, could not fail to accomplish any task that met the hands. There should not be the strain on the belief of this one in attempting to accomplish any task the hand findeth to do. There could be the healing of the sick. There could be even the raising of the dead with that presence that is in the heart of this one and the realization of the closeness to Him that was the Master. For this one was especially close to Jesus who became the Christ, and helped in teaching Him in His younger days when there were the retreats on the mountains of Carmel. There was the walking with Him in the garden and beside the rivers, and the talking with Him of those disciplines that you would call the mystic, those disciplines in which He was tested in the Egyptian lands.

There was the walking with this one with John, who is called in your scriptures John the Baptist, the Harbinger. There was the acquaintance between this one and Elizabeth, the mother of the harbinger, and with Mary, the mother of the Christ. And if there would be for this one the studying of the scriptures and the quiet times at night, and if there would be the turning inward and turning backward, there would be the remembrance of walking with this Man. And there would be in the heart the seeing of this Man even in this moment, as a man wearing a pearl grey robe all of one piece flowing about Him, with steel blue, piercing eyes, with the dark reddish eyebrows, with the beard that parts in the center and has two peaks coming down from the chin. The hair would be seen as a very deep, rich, wine red, the color of new wine, flowing down to the shoulders and curling about the shoulders. The fingers would be seen as long and tapered, and you would see on this small finger of the left hand one long nail, which always was worn long.

Now attempt to reconstruct this man of ruddy features, a muscular man, one who was very much a man, very masculine, one whose eyes were piercing but kind, one whose voice spoke with authority. Realize that there were even the times that He came to thee for the teaching. Now not that this one would be built up inside by the knowledge of these things or the remembrance of these things. But how could one help but be humbled by knowledge of being so close to the Divine? And how great a burden in this lifetime to realize the responsibility of being one so blessed.

Now be aware of that which dwells within. For if there were the awareness, if there were the use of the power that lies within this heart, it would be seen as true that no one even could touch the garments of this one without being helped. Be aware of all that goes on about you. Be aware of how many thousands of people you will touch during your lifetime. And would it stagger the imagination to realize it if that many people would be helped by your touch? But it is true. It cannot fail. It is the word of God. It is given to all His servants, not only to this one.

This has come as an example that the world may know that it is true, that all are one in Christ and there is no limit to the Christ power. That which is the Christ force is available to all. Thou art a storehouse of energy yet untapped that has come this night that this catalyst may be the unleashing of this energy that has been stored up for so long. Not that this one would go out in a frenzy of activity, attempting to spread about the Christ energy throughout the world. The best that you can do for Christ is to relax and be.

But be aware that "All power is given unto Me both in Heaven and in Earth." In His words go you therefore, and preach the gospel to all nations, to every creature, baptizing them in the name of the Father, the Son, and the Holy Ghost. And He has spoken, "Lo, I am with you always, even unto the end of the Earth". This promise is true this night for He is present in this room and is aware of your presence and repeats the promise, "I am with you always."

Now thou canst not fail in any situation to be of help when the hand is extended and the attitude of help, the seeking to be of service. For He seeks even yet to be of service, and He cannot fail. Thou art but an instrument in His hand. See self in this manner, and attempt to be a tool of service.

Now we would see this one surrounded by the golden light, and in the aura there are the ruffles, the furls, the ribbons of white; and flowing down about the body are the rays of pink. There is a great deal of blue rising as it were from the Earth in this aura to complete that which would be the outline of this body. And we would seek that this one would dress in this manner: that the tops in particular could be the combinations of the gold, the white and the delicate pink. The skirts, or that which would be worn on the lower portion of the body would be blue, a rich healthy blue, and there may be the manifestations of pink in the total garment, and of green in all the garments when there is the seeking to be of service in healing, or when there is the seeking of healing to be brought within this body. For the deep rich forest greens may be manifested in this aura, may be called to the service when they are needed.

Be aware that when this one prays for the healing of self or for another there will not be refused the request. This one would, with even a kernel of belief, … say with the Apostle Paul, "I can do all things through Christ, who is my strength." There are no limitations to the power of this one, except as put on self. This is the message that thou will then preach to others, that this is universally true. There are no limits, except within self.

Now as a stone that may be worn about the neck for this one, that would be the expression of all that is in this heart and life, and on the finger of this one particularly would be the opal. That expression of color and white, the combinations of color to produce the white light, the expressions of the integrations of the forces of this world.

Now as to the questions that have been brought, it is given that this one should not bear children in this lifetime, that here would be the complications and a great deal of difficulty. There would be the danger in attempting this in this lifetime. It is given that there will come into the life one, a charge from God, that should be raised. That will be the purpose for this incarnation. And seek to teach him as thou did in the former incarnation when thou wert holy and blessed. And seek that he will carry the ministry of the Christ force in this world, for this one will be a special servant of Mine. It is given that you would not look for this experience, for it will come unbidden. Pray to be made worthy of this one who is given as a charge, and watch and wait for this opportunity. It is given only as you develop to receive him.

Now the questions as asked concerning the healing in this lifetime. And it has [been] answered and has been given in this manner, that these prayers would be the realization that the healing has already begun. At the moment that there is the touch of thy hands upon the brow of him that is diseased, the healing has begun. And realize this, take it for granted, and go thy way, caring not what the day may bring. For the healing will come in the manner in which God would see it to be sent. That is, one may be released into the inner planes, or may pass on from your lifetime, but this would be the manifestation of healing. And realize that healing does not exist, does not manifest on the physical plane. But on the higher levels, that healing is begun here. And whether or not it descends into the physical level and manifests there is not the importance of the healing. For the conditions are given for the growth experiences of the soul. Seek then that the healing would take place within the soul. And realize that it has been done as thou hast spoken, when there is the request of this one who is so close.

Now there is the turmoil in the heart of this particular seeker in this moment. And it is seen from these planes that there is the realization that it is very difficult to adjust to what has been said this night, that thou art a very special one. But it will be easier if there will be the realization within this heart, saying, "You and I are one" to all that are about. All who are God's people are special. This one has had a very special incarnation, and has been very close with the Master, and carries very special gifts.

But realize within the heart that this is only a humbling experience. It is the great burden, and is realized from this plane the great burden in manifesting in such a way. But realize as well the great opportunities, that it is not possible that [if] you would smile on one of the children that they will not be blessed.

Now believe this, and see it occur. See the miracles of God in your daily life and realize that this one in particular can raise the entire race a little [closer] to the Godhead by the manifestation of her life. This one, by the walking of her steps, could change the positions of the stars in the heavens. See the Master, for He is near. In this moment, you can reach out and touch Him.

Now go, thou blessed of the Father, and manifest His life among the children. And know that He will never leave or forsake thee, but will assist in every work thy hand findeth to do. We are through for now.

#5003 (10-27-72)

EXCERPT 38

Conductor: You have before you (1016). He comes seeking his relationship to the universal forces, to his work, and to this Fellowship.

Yes, we see the questions of this heart. Now we would give that which has been withheld, that this one might realize the purpose and understand those feelings that are inherent within the heart. And we have long awaited opportunity to express that which this heart would wonder concerning those moments that could even pass through the memory in this day, when there was the unspoken but understood promise of the Master, Jesus, that again they would visit together. For this is the beloved Gaius, who was a Greek mercenary, and in the service of Pontius Pilate – one of those who witnessed the trial of the Christ and one who even walked with Him toward that hill, the "Place of the Skull" [Golgotha]. And this one stood even on the court of the home of the high priest when the Prophet of the Jewish people was so abused by His own. The confusion stood then in this heart. And there was the disgust for this nation that he saw as superstitious and emotional – and there was rejection of the Christ Himself.

This one stood in awe of the manhood of the man, Jesus, and was impressed by His manner, as through the ordeal He was calm and serene. And this one noted with amazement that never did there pass even across His face, nor in His eyes, any look of fear or any temptation toward anger, nor did He ever seem to lose control of the situation. And this one could bear witness, even in this day, that the high priest himself, in facing the man Jesus, was intimidated and frightened, and lashed out, almost as if in self-protection, at a man who apparently stood helpless but [was] masterfully in control of all that occurred. And this heart, even in this day, bears witness to those words that are not recorded, but this one knows the composure that was the man, Jesus, as He went before Pontius Pilate. And this one is aware in his heart that the man Pilate had no choice, nor did the others about, for the Christ was in control of all that occurred that night.

This one could remember the journey to the "Place of the Skull," only about two miles distant from the place of the trial, and could recall those moments when the wrists of the Master were nailed to the tree, and watched His face in those moments. And it would seem natural for this one to know, though others would deny and not understand, that it was with a smile and blessing on those about that He carried His cross. And, unlike those two who were crucified, that He was not held to His cross, but lay Himself on it, and willingly spread His arms, and accepted the spikes without flinch of pain. And it was in those moments when the spikes were driven through the wrists that the eyes met, for this one deeply searched the face of the Christ for expression of pain or regret. And it was as if in answer to an unasked question that the Christ looked up into his eyes and said: "No, I will not yield."

This one observed as the cross was raised into the air, held over the pit provided, and even dropped into place with the wrists nailed thereto. And he watched for expression of defeat, but there was none. And again the face of the Christ expressed, as He looked upon him, "I am victorious, even in this hour." It would be known that this one watched and the turmoil of the heart increased as he saw the blessing from the Master pronounced on all those who came about. And he saw the One hanging on the tree, reassuring the followers who seemed to suffer more than He. And it was this one who took the reed with a sponge, in response to the request of thirst, and dipping it in vinegar and gall for purpose of relieving the pain, he offered it to the lips of Christ. It was with a smile that He refused, as if to say: "I endure pain with no relief."

It was at the cross that the decision was made in this heart that there existed, in this man, a Power greater than that he knew. And it was in that moment after the soul had left the body – when the earth began to shake, the sky turned black as pitch, and the waters ran, the graves of the dead cracked open, and there was much fear in other hearts – this one stood, looked upon the cross, and vowed to be a servant of Him.

This one heard the preachings of Paul. And was blessed by the Beloved John, and was very close, often serving him and protecting him in his latter days. And it is for this reason that even in this day, this one feels drawn in his heart toward that city where they met and walked together. And as he serves and prepares self, so will the way be provided that he may meet and walk again with the beloved servant John and assist in his latter day.

And the question would be here, "If I am to teach, if I am to serve, why am I not given that gift of expression and the education that would make it convenient for me to tell that which I feel in my heart?" And the answer would be given in this way: Thy purpose was to be a man, even as He was a man. And the prompting in this life is to overcome all that is of the flesh and to speak that which would be of Him.

This one is well aware that he would not, that he could not, depend on semantics, or the words of an educated tongue. But if he would speak inspired words of the Divine, they must come from on High. Learn then to so give the instrument of thy lips to His command. Then thou couldst speak words of the Christ. Those words of encouragement, of instruction, of love. And if there would be the giving of self to His service so completely, thou wouldst then become the instrument through which nought would be expressed but love. And would not He live again this day, and would not the Earth hear His voice, if such an instrument, if such lips, were given?

There will be then opportunity to preach, if this one would boldly set himself in that position, to preach the words of the Master. Then asking, open the lips to speak. And as you expect Him to speak, so will He speak, even through thine instrument. For this one has been visited by the servant John, and is aware of his touch, his blessing, even in this lifetime, and has communicated with him. Be aware that it is so. This is for the blessing, that thou might understand and hast been given a ministry. And know that "All power is Mine, in Heaven and in Earth." And in His words, go ye therefore, for thou art commissioned to do the work of the Christ in this world. He has set you apart with a blessing and given you all that is needed for the construction of His work.

Now there are the many lessons to be learned. And thou art given patience. And thou art given opportunity in this place that is set before you. And as you would see opportunity for service, so shall you serve. And thy service shall be measured in the progress that is seen in this place, that which you would produce with what God has provided. Then build a place of worship, build a temple of service, and that which you shall do shall be blessed.

Know that He would walk with thee in the development of those abilities, as has been given. And it is the request of the Master that we would have this one realize that often would He walk with thee, if thou wouldst become still. And know that those joyous experiences that have come will seem as nought when His touch would be known. For that baptism of fire would surpass earthly emotion. And words cannot express what thou shalt experience in that moment when personality is given [up] and His life becomes thine.

Now thou art grown into a shepherd. Feed His sheep. We are through for now.

#1016-2 (2-6-73)

EXCERPT 39

Conductor: You have before you (9001), born November 9, 1936 in Tift County, Georgia. She comes seeking information concerning her past lives and her relationship to the universal forces.

Yes, we have these records. Now there are the many lifetimes that may be brought here that would increase the awareness, the understanding of those pressures, those problems of this time. But for those that would bring most understanding, we would have this one see in this manner that thou were present in those days when there were the persecutions following the time when the Master walked the earth. And you were present and saw those persecutions when Stephen and the others there with him were stoned. And it was you who looked into the eyes of the young man, Saul, with an accusing look that first caused his mind to turn from thinking and produced the guilt as he stood holding the cloaks, the coats of those doing the stoning. And it was in those moments that he dropped these coats to the ground, and taking his animal, his beast of burden, left this group for the accusing look that was in thine eyes.

And the name in that time was Ophelia. And there was the confusion in the heart for the lack of understanding. For ye were not of the Hebrew faith or nationality, but mixed Roman and Greek. And not understanding the religious laws, there was confusion why one, a Jew, would stand and even assist in the stoning, the killing of another, for religious reasons and convictions. And you saw the face, the countenance of Stephen and Illia and the others here as they were transformed and their faces became as the faces of angels. And it was with interest that you watched those Christians as their zeal, their ardor grew. And it was only some three years following that you met with an underground group, and the one you had seen and accused stood before thee to preach the gospel of His name. The one Saul had become Paul. And you went away not understanding. Yet there were the times following when you accepted.

And that you might understand those persecutions of this present lifetime, we would have you know that there was the birth in the land of the present nativity in the year of 1659, and the name Ellen J. Reed, the nativity then in Watertown, Massachusetts. And this was one [who was] very strict in the religious beliefs, very judgmental concerning the beliefs of others, one very straight-laced and demanding, one who looked too much into the lives of others and accused. And in those times when there were the accusations of witchcraft, and such persecutions, it was known that you had seen visions, that you had prophesied in the church of that day. And there came from the hands great heat for healing.

[And you], for the protection of self, accused others, causing them to suffer. And so has it been turned against you in this lifetime, that you were in that day somewhat a Sadducee, self-righteous, condemning others for their lack of ability to live up to that which thou wouldst preach. And in this lifetime hast thou not suffered the same? And know that thy daughters are among those persecuted by thee in that time. But that understanding has come, that adjustment has been made. And it is with pleasure that we would come in this time, and help you to understand that which has been owed has been paid and that which you build will be to thy benefit.

Now there are the other times that might be of interest, and the other teachings that could be given. And that which you would wonder here concerning the closeness, the feeling of protectiveness toward this channel, comes from the lifetime in Egypt, when you were the mother of the priest Il Kammon, and brought him up in such ways that he was prepared and became the learned one, the leader of all his people.

9001-2 (5-29-73)

EXCERPT 40

Yes, we have this body and the life of this entity, and those questionings concerning the directions for this lifetime, and those purposes, or that which comes as influence in the life at this time. And we would have you see in this manner, as has been given, that as there are the seekers who would attune, as there are the souls that have come into being on these planes, there is for each soul a pattern of evolvement; i.e., there is, for each soul, a system that has been planned. And it has been given according to your scripture that there are the "Books" in which the souls are recorded. It might be seen, metaphorically, in this manner, that as [there are the] many stars in the universe, and [as] many as [are] the grains of sand upon the shores of all the seas, even so, there are so many systems that have been set into being, [and] there are as many lessons, as many situations, as many systems, for the teaching of each single [soul] as would be needed for the attunement. Unless there would be the opening of the heart at this moment, there is not the possibility for the human mind to understand that which has been stated.

But passing aside the narrowness of your mind, we would have you see in this manner that that which we attempt to state is this: that there have been those who have looked at this one and said, "You have not arrived at this point by the method by which we arrived at this point; therefore, you are not of us." There has been the questioning as well, in the heart of this one, as to "Which of these others have arrived at the point that I have arrived at?"

And we would have it understood, in all these hearts, that each of you is a perfect expression of the perfect God in His perfect world. And you have reached your own unique point in growth, in discipline, in development, in the body of God. These disciplines are given you that you might fit into that point in His system, in His body, to do that job for which you were perfected! And let it be known that he among you who would say, "I wish his job, or I would like to have the talent that this one has, or that one has," in so doing, would pray for imperfection. For there has been spent lifetime after lifetime perfecting you, your body, your soul, your mind, for the situation in which you would fit at this time, for the purpose for which you are to serve. All talents are given by the Master, and are given for a purpose. No one else can do the job you have been sent to do.

#1016 (1-7-73)

Sex & Related Topics

EXCERPT 41

As to morality in regard to sex, those acts are wrong that disappoint others in your relation to them – for example, those acts that would cause a person who deeply loves and trusts another entity to be unfaithful to that one he loves. Those acts are wrong that are not shared in love. Those acts are wrong that are selfish. Those acts are good, however, that cause a sharing between two souls. The perfection of love is in making one another happy in whatever manner this may be obtained. It is good and blessed. It is the selfishness of an act that makes it wrong.

Therefore, enter into what you do with another entity with love in your heart and with his satisfaction as your goal. Make it as a sharing together and it is right – remembering, however, as has been stated, that that act is wrong which disappoints the other person in his own principles or his principle of faithfulness to a loved one.

2402 (3-1-72)

EXCERPT 42

How many on this plane who are of manifestation could overcome the body, the flesh, if we could allow you to understand these principles? But understand those laws, for this becomes such mishmash within the mind, and these become boggled in that they dare not think through or examine. But let your service be on those levels that would cause acceptance, and let that acceptance be given on those levels that are acceptable, each to one another. Learn to express love in such a way that will not leave doubt in the heart of one. And as he would see himself accepted in such a real, in such a loving way, in the Christian manner through service one to the other, so he would not find so great a need to use the physical body or the lower self as expression of love. Then equate love with the higher expressions, and so overcome.

Now we have spoken of that force that has been raised. And understand that when spiritual development would begin, there would come the turning on those lowest levels of the physical, or within the creative urge that is equated with the sexual and which stimulates those glands. So there would be that which you have seen in spiritual development and has been a problem through the ages. For in that very earliest day of spiritual growth or awakening, there begins in the seeker the desire to deal with the sexual urge. This first then calls to the attention.

Now understand, this has been described as inordinate attention to the smallest, the least of the laws. But understand the reason for the occurrence. For the beginning of spiritual growth is the beginning of power. And as it would begin to unleash within the body, so it would call attention to these centers, these organs. Then would it not be natural that such would gain the immediate attention of those seeking to develop spiritually? So there would come then the struggle to deal with this single problem. And so many, never growing past that raising of the first center, then remain with attention called to such lower levels.

Then what would be the answer and what would lift these in spiritual growth? See it in this manner, even as we have described: Begin then giving attention to the higher levels of the body, using this energy, this force, this power. For it is a very real force and power. And if you desire the ability to create, to heal, to project, to accomplish on this plane, then use that power. But use it for creative purposes, for that which you wish to create. For in the act of such it is released, or that power is unleashed. And for what purpose? To give only pleasure? And if so, then pleasure. But if that desire is for creativity, then use that power, use that energy raised to those levels, that there might be the developing of such. For it is this energy, this power and this alone that can be raised in these centers of the body to direct the body or the understanding for a purpose to build.

Then it would not be any surprise among you that so many never accomplish that which has been described, even from these records, as potential. For many have been told there that you possess the ability to make this accomplishment, that accomplishment. And some seem so great they could seem almost to be fantasized, even from these planes.

And why would it be so? There is not any man among you, there is not one living on that plane of Earth that, were he to harness the power of his physical body and that given to him to be directed, could not heal your land, could not raise the consciousness of this nation. Then these are not exaggerated as they are given. They are given in challenge. They are given in seeing that power that lies dormant, as it might be described, at the base of the spine. They are given as seeing that power raised to its highest level within the human body. And so there is no limit to that which might be accomplished through all among you.

Then would we condemn those who give the self in sexual satisfaction? Not condemnation, not from these records, not from our purposes. Yet see what would be your purpose. And if your purpose be pleasure, then pleasure. And so will these forces be released, for such purpose. But if your purpose then would be spiritual growth, would be accomplishment, would be creativity, then channel those energies to those higher centers that would be given, that would be dedicated for such purpose.

Can you speak about marriage? And it has been given and taught through many of the masters in those writings that have been recorded, that there is given the release among those who would seek to develop and are on the path, for co-creation and not for pleasure even in marriage. And if there would be the raising of the level of consciousness, then let them withhold for that time and raise that energy that would be required and directed for a purpose, and let them accomplish. Not that these then even in marriage would become celibate, for this is not necessary, for these can be raised and used. Then there can be the release within the physical body, if given for purpose and direction. And even in this act, in this manner, can there be the sharing between two souls.

Is it not written, even in your scripture, that it would be better for the man to cast his seed into the belly of a whore than to spill it upon the ground? See then for this reason that these should be brought together in the sharing one with another and giving of that energy of self, all that is of the body, between the two people rather than the releasing for no purpose.

Then understand that these bodies have been given as tools, as equipment, and that man who would learn to control his vehicle, that man who would learn to drive the automobile with all its power, to harness this engine directed exactly to that place that he would want to go. See the analogy then. Understand the body in this way. You are a soul, having been placed in a vehicle on this plane to learn to deal with the laws of this plane. Then if you would spend all that energy that is given in pleasure, then what would you accomplish but pleasure?

If that energy then is directed for a purpose, then what would be your purpose? What wouldst thou accomplish? What would you name? What could you name? Would you heal the sick? Would you raise the dead? Would you build cities? Would you move mountains? "All power is given unto Me, both in Heaven and Earth." This spoken by the Son of God, not the Father. And art thou not the Son? And being the Son of God, have you less power than Him who spoke? But know all power is given unto thee both in Heaven and Earth. And if you would learn then to harness that power to use as energy, then so it would be accomplished.

4031 (7-24-73)

EXCERPT 43

Conductor: What is God's law concerning the sex life of single or divorced persons?

Now understand in the bringing of these laws or the understanding of these, first that there might be the examining of purposes for the institution of laws in any manner about this plane or about the physical or the universal – speaking for this reason that all appetites given to man are for the health and for the growth of man or that of the individual. Then so it is with the expression of sex – that these are for the health, for the growth and are the natural process.

Now if there would be the greater understanding of that occurring within sex we would see these manufactured in the body, not only of the gland, but of those energy centers or vortexes or that of the soul – the etheric body – as would correspond with these gland levels, and would be of a common type or stimulation, you see, that these are created in the nature. Then that happening within the soul force or the ideal force of self, corresponding on the higher with that manifesting on the physical as the lower, then the physical act as itself, would prevent the higher act of the soul from taking place.

Now these are intended then for the bringing together of self with an opposite polarity of self, or with another soul in the expression of two together. There can be then, in these expressions, the expression of the highest within the self, or the blessing of one another. Or in the purely physical, can be the use of one another.

Now this we would find pleasing or displeasing [to] the highest within the self, that manner of partaking of same. If the expression is the lower or animal nature, so will be the reaction, and will bring the self to manifesting the lower or animal nature in other things that are done. If the purpose then is in the worship, or the expression of the highest within the self, or the healing, or the love manifestation, so then it will bring too higher levels within the self.

If there would be the expression sexually then in those who are single – [remember] that the laws were given that there might be [sexual relations] among only the married for the reason that the committal of self to bring that body together with another would be for the completion of self for the lifetime. Then there should be the commitment to another if there would be the entering into the sexual act, not for the moment, but for the eternity, or for that lifetime on this plane. [There] should be some commitment to serving one another within the purposes, for there is the joining together here of the physical, of the bodies you see, and cannot be separated again. Once there is the spilling of one into another, these have been brought together and would contain those karmic lessons one of the other. And no possibility that you would take that that is a secretion of the physical body and place in the physical body of another without making that continual bond for that entire lifetime between these two physical bodies. Then you are joined karmically in that need, with as many as you have given the self into. Now whether there be the exchange of the sputum or the semen, if there is the exchange of fluids from one body to another, there has been the form of karmic bond.

Then that as was the thought, or the purposes, the intent of the self in that time of exchange, would be that given to another. If that I had given to that body then was given as blessing, as love, as desire to see this one develop into the higher, then I have sent this or projected this into the body.

Now we speak not only in those activities of the entry or the penetration. We speak as well of the spilling in other manners of the sex here, or any time there is the release of the self or the orgasm, that climax of one to the other. That that would be of the nature of self or the thought or the purpose in entering into the relationship, here will be that formed.

Understand then the physical act is only a physical act. That mental, that spiritual within the self would be that that would be judged by the self or by thy God. Then see the intents, the purposes of entering any act.

Now as there be the examining of intent or purpose within the self, this must be considered the other, or understand here that such an act would require the two. And examine those intents and purposes of the other with whom you join in that act. If this one then with whom you enter must be unfaithful to one to whom he is committed, then you have brought a third into that karmic lesson, or have formed karmic bonds with that partner or the one that the other is obligated to in that way, so that there is formed a bond here between the three that must be settled or considered in the life or throughout eternity. Then understand that if there be the entering into such a bond, that both must be free of obligation to another.

Then if there would be the producing in the other or in the self the feeling of guilt or regret, then this must be considered as that I have taken of myself. If I would cause another to regret that act he has taken with me, I owe then that I must give myself in such a way in return to him, or I will be used by him in those periods that come. Understand those lessons of karma in this way. All these then must be considered in the giving of self.

This is the reason that it has been spoken by the masters that "Unless there would be given of myself for the lifetime to another, I would not give so much of myself as the issue of my seed into his body or hers." Understand this. There is the forming of a bond that cannot be broken in the bringing together of two physical bodies in this way. Not a situation to be taken lightly.

Then for [those who are] single, best that you spill the seed upon the ground or stimulate the self or allow these to come into the periods of night if there would be the spilling forth. Yet better that you bring those periods of understanding or those periods of stimulation in this way and give forth to another in love or in healing, or use these in creativity.

Now understand that same energy that is spilled forth from the body in those sexual acts is that exact same energy that would be used in the creation of art, of craft, of activity of creation in this way. Know that greater creativity may be brought if there is the use of this, or the bringing up through the body.

Now if there would be for the single man or the single woman that use of these in this way, there may be the stimulating of self, even manually as we would see, or the stimulating of the sexual organs to that extent that there is arousal or production of energy in that of the lower chakra. Then as there is the praying, bring the hands to point to each of those chakras, bringing this energy up, dedicating this to higher purpose. Then you will find the self to experience the orgasm, as it were, on seven different levels, yet not the spilling forth of seed at all. There would be the convulsing of the muscles at each of these seven chakras and on those seven levels. And there will be that greater experience that could be experienced on a single level, you see, if these be brought to the higher.

In such a way will that spirit, will that mind be stimulated to the higher activity that may be used for higher purposes or for the healing. Study that manner in which such are brought by those of the yogis or those who have prepared themselves in such way and have gained such control over the body.

Now we state not in a moralistic way that there should not be activity between those single. Yet we do say here that the manner of those teachings of the masters was given for the reason that there is knowledge that there is formed karmic bond in the giving of one to another. Take only these things into consideration as you express the self. And knowing such laws, take these and dedicate the self to the Father. Then proceed with that that self, the highest within the self, would allow that you do.

1035 (10-15-73)

EXCERPT 44

A short time [ago], there were asked those questions of how can we overcome sin? How can we resist temptation? How can we be stronger, to be sure that we will not yield to temptation in our daily lives? And there was an answer given in words from this source, and yet there was a greater answer given this day in thine experience.

Now which teaches the more – that which is told you or that which thou would experience in your own daily life? We learn more from experience. And it would seem this day that because the heart and mind were filled with things of God, the temptations slid [by] almost unnoticed, almost as if they did not exist. Yet, the same temptations were there. The temptations that you would face on your job day-by-day – the opportunity to sin, to slip and use the Lord's name in the wrong way, the opportunity to anger, the opportunity to disgust, and all these other things were present today. But because God was so much more present, these opportunities for sin slipped by unnoticed.

Would not then those angels in Heaven even now rejoice? Even as they rejoiced as one who was lost came before the throne, so they rejoice when one who is His child, His lamb, finds victory in growing in Christ.

This then is the one means of overcoming sin, of overcoming temptation in the world: to have present in thy mind the things of God, the love of God, the realization of the power of God. This is the overcoming of sin. Then we would further apply these things in this manner. For when there is the temptation that comes, then how do we overcome it?

In the close intimate relationship between the two lovers, there is the temptation as you would say to let the hands wander, to let the mind wander, to become involved. Then as these things become temptation and we would be drawn to sin, then how do we overcome it? We would find this. You yourself bring on yourself temptation, in continuing those things we know produce temptation. For in the moment that you are together and share together a love in Christ, and you look upon her beauty, and in your heart you thank God for giving you this one, how can you sin? How can there be sin in that relationship?

Then in the next moment when thou hast taken this one in thy arms, thou still can rejoice. This is a gift of God – that close relationship together, the enjoying of each other, of one another, and the sharing together. And as long as this one is in thine arms and thou still can say in thy heart God has given you to me and I praise Him and I love you through Him, then this is a blessed relationship.

Then as it is allowed to go further and further, there comes what you know as a stimulation. Then with this comes the temptation to sin, for the thoughts are drawn from God and drawn to the physical. Then how do we overcome this?

Realize this. The temptation in itself is not sin. Temptation is the opportunity to sin. Strength comes then in overcoming temptation. Where is the wisdom then? The wisdom is in this. Know where that point stops that thou art praising God for a loved one and where that point begins where the earthly desires, the desires of the flesh, take over and draw toward sin and away from God. At that point, turn thy thoughts then back to God. Look on thy loved one as a gift and say, "Thank you God for giving me this." Then share together love in God, and the temptation towards sin is taken away.

How then can we continue day-by-day helping men abstain from those things of sex? How can we put those things away from our minds and grow instead to loving God?

Know in this that thou hast made a schedule. And in following that schedule will be the daily exercise. And the mind then will be taken up in things of God. And there will not be time for the temptation. For when does the temptation toward sex come? If you will think, it comes at those times when there is the relaxation. The mind is wandering. And through not thinking of the things of God, through not exercising the mind in this one problem, this one study or another, there comes in the empty or the idle mind, those thoughts of sin. And this brings the temptation to the fall.

Then if thy mind art kept busy on things of God, on studying and learning the things of God, and praising God, whence comes the temptation to sin? And if the physical body is kept busy and tired, and release is given through exercise, then that stimulation is overcome in this manner. And the body does not crave the release through sex. For this then in the human body is a substitute for physical exercise and can be worked off in other ways.

Now there still will come those times of stimulation, those times when there should be the sexual release. These things then, if left alone and handled in nature's way, will be handled by themselves. For when have you experienced nocturnal emission, this will come, if you leave alone the physical things that bring that simulation. For those glands will release themselves, but they will be released in nature's way, which is God's way, automatically. And will be released without the physical sin. For thy mind and thy heart will be on God during the waking hours, and the exercise will take care of the body, and the mental exercise will take care of the mind. And thy body and thy mind will remain pure in the Lord. Then you might present before Him that body that is a living sacrifice, holy, acceptable unto God.

2414 (4-9-72)

EXCERPT 45

We would find that in these early times, in the very earliest times of Atlantis and Mu, these groups of souls had come as androgynous beings, all of a common type, or not polarized but containing both positive and negative polarity. Or though the terms are inadequate, [these beings] could be described as male and female in the single body. These came not for production and were not given to reproduction, but had come in curiosity, for the experience of creativity and recreation. And it became the experience of these early souls that through projecting the thoughts – for these entered first as thought forms – they projected for themselves vehicles of animal type, then entering into these vehicles, these thought forms, that then became capable of reproduction in animal fashion. Now it might be described, though this would be analogy and inadequate in words of your language, that all these would be seen as male or the positive.

Now we give description in this way only because these were the creative force, and not male or masculine in the sense of the masculine body. Yet these as thought forms, creators and co-creators with the Father, were able to provide themselves with alternate thought forms of opposite polarity, or distinguish the polarity within the self [by] separating the self from an opposite side of self, thus giving an inferior. Now we would see in this manner as it occurred, that the positive or creative force became the greater, and that which he provided as receptacle for himself became the lesser in his thinking, and he dominated the other.

In such a manner were those first souls or soul mates formed from a single body, these [separated] then, being the receptacles, not necessarily the female in the sense of your time, yet the underlings or the created beings. Now these might have been equipped in the physical sense as the male, yet that one that was created from the other or became lesser than the master, the creator, became a race unto itself, so that these were considered inferior beings and became beasts of burden or servants to that one the creator.

Now in the giving of selves to reproduction, or in the attempts to reproduce in animal fashion and bring other souls into existence, it became the choice of the creator to cause the childbearing to be done by the inferior breed. In such a manner came those thoughts of the female being [considered] the lesser within the human race.

Now these were not as you would see the female, and had not at that time developed as human or in the perfected vehicle. Yet in those times of Atlantis were these unfortunate creatures used by the creator, so beginning those cycles of karma between the male and the female. And we would see that in the adjusting or the righting of that which was created in that time, there must come in these days a rule of the female. Or that is, that the female will become the superior and will dominate the race, the male, before the ending of this time, for the righting of that which has been created, and we see the beginnings of this in this time.

Now to understand the role of that seeker who comes this night, we would understand that she was one of those born as child to that considered the inferior or the second half of the creator body. There came then a breed of those, these children, that in growing up recognized that which had occurred and saw that these, although created, were not inferior to that one from whose body they were created. And so began that first campaign for the rights of human beings as might be called, though such were not as such at that time.

Now these were the times given to the perfecting of the physical bodies and to the creating of that that would become the perfect vessel, the perfect temple for the manifestation of man. And these were the times when the Sons of God entered this plane to bless those daughters of men, so raising that level, so perfecting that vehicle.

And if there would be realized the purposes for coming in this time, we would see that, [like] so many, that purpose or ideal would be for the balance, or the not giving to a particular ideal or idea, or giving of self entirely to one principle, but for the bringing all together of that which has been accomplished, that which has been realized, that which championed a cause.

For this one saw much of the development in Atlantis and the coming of those times that the race, begun as androgynous or single, one with the Father and worshiping the Law of One, had become a polarized race, or a race worshiping rather duality, a race of extremes. So it is in this time, [with] so many having developed as extremes or having widened the gap even, between the male and the female over the periods of time.

And we use these illustrations as male and female because we find such in the mind of the seeker. Yet this quality, this polarity exists not only in the separation of the sexes, but in the feelings of polarity with the Father, between the races, between ideas, so even as developed in those times of the Atlanteans, causing the destruction of those isles. And we would find that the reason for destruction was polarity, or the development of extremes within the people. For these separated themselves into the sons and daughters of the law of One, as opposed to the sons and daughters of Belial. And because of their polarity, because of the separation, because of insistence on following extremes, so did their times, their land become destroyed.

Now find those symptoms in your culture. And rather than widening the gap, instead of developing polarity, emphasize that the purpose of those coming in at this time then [is] to bring those sexes back to one. For it is in your time that the planet Adam will appear. And [by] those bodies now given to one polarity or another, and those minds so separated by tradition, by type, by that which is taught – that this is the female mind, this is the male mind – there will be learned that the soul is not male or female. But that as it is developed and comes together within itself or [in the] completing [of] itself and its cycles, so it becomes balanced and is androgynous. And there is chosen for a vehicle from time to time that most suitable to the development, and should not be thought of as "I am male, or I am female."

These ideas should be discarded in this time, for they are obsolete and were given as thoughts only that there might be the populating of those lands, and were chosen by man. Or that is, it might be described as not the idea of God, but man's own creation that he should separate self into polarity, causing there to be the male, the female for purposes of reproduction. For God's idea in creation was creation, or that man should be co-creator with God and not using those methods of animals for reproduction, but speaking into life or breathing the breath of life into that vehicle produced from the self. So would all have given birth directly from their own bodies. But it was the cowardice, as might be described, of the male – and these words come from one called Fortune, in describing that manner that such task or job was delegated to one of lower species in that time – so that one giving birth from her own body became known as the lower of the species through the cowardice of that creator who failed in his task.

So all these will return then to this singularity, or the bringing of androgynous souls into androgynous bodies in this time, and is for the purpose of ending duality on this plane. And as you would negate duality between the sexes, so in the same act will ye negate duality between good and evil. So will you begin to realize the self as God and be lifted from this plane of manifestation and duality to the plane of His presence and light.

1040 (4-13-73)

EXCERPT 46

We would delight to satisfy that which is the wondering of all these hearts concerning these matters of birth, of the entering of the soul into your plane. And understand these things, that it be for your spiritual edification, that even through this description you might understand that virgin birth of the Master. For it was in this wise, even as this one has come this night, that these things operate according to natural universal laws, which are the laws of God. And in those cycles of the woman and in her heart, there are those conditions created by the feelings, the emotions, the thought forms, in cooperation with those natural cycles of the body. So that in production of that which is called the egg or the seed here, in the female body, there is the realization within the auric field, or that field of force, that life field surrounding the body, there is the awareness of such conditions of productivity. And these have been spoken of from these planes as the glow about the life force.

Now such a glow might be produced in prayer. Such a glow might be produced in service, in learning, any of those activities that would cause a change in the electrical force field about the body, as a result of changing awareness. Now there are the changes that are brought about by disease, there are those changes brought about by the healing, there are the changes brought about by those natural cycles of life, and each would produce its glow.

Now understand that from the planes of the inter-between, or from those levels in which spirits would exist, that these which you would know as uncarnate or discarnate are those awaiting those cycles of life that they might re-enter this birth plane. And those who have passed and are about to go to higher levels, these are aware not of the body, not of the material which you would inhabit, not of the physical, but only of the glow that is produced. Then you might understand that these are attracted to those who produce the spiritual glow, hence some among you are known as mediums or those who would attract the spirit forces. Now in such a manner such a glow is produced during the periods of prayer, the periods when the heart, the soul is crying out, calling out to spirit, and attracting those on other planes that they might be brought for service or for comfort. Just in such a way are many among you possessed or obsessed with these dealings of spirit, the knowledge of spirit, the crossing of the veil as it were, or the sudden lifting of the veil, in such a way as might produce fear, as might produce obsession with things of spirit.

Now we bring all these things that you might understand that which happens at the time of conception. For there is, in the female, the glow that is produced at that time that the egg, or that which is the receptacle, would be released in these cycles of the body. Now understand that this will produce a measurable difference in that current which passes through the force field about the body and then would produce the glow. It is at that time, even prior to the entering of the seed, or the sperm from the male, that there are attracted those spirits from the plane of the inter-between. Then if there be those spirits that are particularly attracted to the mother and with whom there is an affinity, then the mother will feel the glow within the subconscious self and will feel desire that this egg, [at] this time, during this cycle, would become fertile. Or that is, might produce a field in which this particular spirit who has an affinity with me, this soul, this person with whom I have karmic ties might use this that my body now is producing. So that it is within the subconscious thinking of the mother, accompanied with that feeling of the spirit who would enter here and would need these karmic conditions or would have an affinity for this spirit. These two then, being compatible, would be drawn together, so that at this time the mother becomes receptive to that seed, that sperm that could come from the male.

Now understand these do not always mean the best conditions. It is no guarantee that a spirit so coming and entering the mother in such a period of time, attracted by that glow produced by this period of the cycle, would be best for that mother. It would only mean that the decision was made by these two souls, or these two who felt they had this in common and were compatible one with the other, that birth might come. These are the conditions then under which conception might take place.

Now be aware that there often are the many souls attracted, or the spirit feels the force fields. And know that that field about the mother, about the father, about all, even in the physical body of this plane, is that same field of that same nature of the one who would enter from the inter-between. So that three are the same here except that two are in the material and produce those conditions that the third might enter.

Now such a thing has occurred in this time, and such a powerful entity here was attracted during this period of the cycle that the mother began to react on subconscious levels because of her affinity, her attraction to the soul attempting to enter on the earth plane at this time. So that even though there was not the preparation, there was not the readiness in the physical existence, in the mental thinking, so that these conditions would have been delayed further.

Yet there is one who has been attracted here who was close with both of these in past incarnations and would seek to incarnate with them here. It is for this reason that so much doubt is produced in the thinking here, thinking that "Even though we had planned to put this away, yet I am attracted and I feel a warmth here. I almost feel as if I would like to let this one enter." And there is confusion as a result of these feelings of the soul, of the deeper levels being incompatible with that which has occurred on the mental level. We would help you then in understanding that that soul that has entered here or has, that we might describe it, tapped thee on the shoulder, requesting entry here, is aware of such conditions and of the need to wait upon these things and to prepare.

Now we would not give from these planes that one should feel guilt for such planning. And there is given from these records no indication that there should be the changing of plans, or the pressure given here that you would continue to carry this and allow such birth. For, as might be described from these records, we would see that that which exists within this body would be only the cellular construction from the body of the mother. We see this not then as a life, as a soul. We see here only a vehicle and a possibility, an opportunity. The choice then is entirely thine. And we would give from these planes that abortion at this time, or the relieving of the body of this potential vehicle, will not be destructive to this system and the bearing may come at a later time, if there would be the desire.

Then pray upon these things and make the decision between you, knowing that conditions are right and "That which we bring about is that which we would love and because we have chosen to do so, and we could create deliberately because we wish this life to come when this life shall come." Under such conditions, there would be again attracted such a soul as needs come in this lifetime and would have an affinity with these two and would share in the spiritual growth. So dedicate the bodies and the thinking to the service of thy God, and bring these in such a manner that you may be of greater service to the Divine and to him who would come, using thy body as a vehicle here.

4003 (5-11-73)

EXCERPT 47

Conductor: [What is the best method of birth control?]

For these in particular we would find little that would be satisfactory. That which is used might be continued. That best would be the bringing of those instruments that would test the electrical cycles of the body. We find these as coming available now, [though] not so available on the market that might be constructed. With a little research you will find that there can be brought here the galvanic skin response tester that will show those cycles when this one would become fertile, and there should be the avoidance then.

Now understand that this would not be the rhythm method, for these cycles cannot be predicted with that accuracy. But there can be tested the response and the knowledge of the level of electrical activity, or the voltage produced in the body of the mother here, with the indication of those times where there is fertility.

4003-2 (5-11-73)

EXCERPT 48

Conductor: Is it possible for a woman to mentally control whether or not she becomes pregnant and how is this done?

We see this not only as possible but often practiced, and it would be the most common control, not only of controlling the birth or avoiding the birth, but also of bringing the birth. It is seldom on your plane that there is an accidental conception – that is, a woman has brought conception within herself, the body has decided and programmed that which would be birth even though the conscious mind of the woman or the couple involved may not have desired it. It should be given as well that even the father may control the birth, even in this manner – that is, that the lack of desire on the part of the father may prevent the conception by producing sterility within himself, and often is done even on your plane.

However, it should be given that there are many factors to be considered in one who would attempt to practice such control for this reason. Fears so often on your plane are subconscious wishes, and where there is a feeling of guilt within a person and a feeling of need to be punished, these things will take the more of punishment and bring into the life that wish the conscious mind would deny as being a desire.

Therefore, there must be the analysis of wishes, of desires, [so] there be the purity within, and the singleness of purpose, the following of Thy will or Divine will within, for Divine will is that which the soul ultimately desires and will bring into the growth process of the soul.

These are the considerations of such control and are ideal situations for control of birth. For that which comes is that which the soul would need. If you would understand then that which would come, be in contact with the soul or that higher part of self. Know self within, and by conquering the law, one becomes the law. And producing the law within self, does not one control the self? The entire body, and all its processes may be controlled in any way by that mind who has become the builder and in control of self.

9006 (1-12-73)

EXCERPT 49

Yes, we have the records and the witnesses of these particular relationships with the universal forces. We would find, in this manner, that for this one there would be two times given for the period of birth. And we would find this not uncommon – that if there were erected the horoscope chart, there would be used the two different birth times, for this reason. We would find that the activity of the body of this entity, or the physical birth, the beginning – that time of the drawing of the first breath, the introducing into this body of the prana of this plane, which would establish the birth time – would be given as 7:59 p.m. However, for the entrance of the soul into this body – that which would gauge the personality or character, particularly the soul qualities, or that position from which the soul came, in entering this body, the understanding of the disciplines learned in the inter-between – would be fixed then on 9:29 p.m. The reason being then that often the entrance of the soul into the physical body in this plane does not necessarily coincide with birth, but is the choice of the soul entity. That relationship which would be formed by the aspects at the moment of the entering of the soul into the body would be the choice of the soul.

6005 (12-16-72)

Soul Development

Conductor: What should we do to grow spiritually?

Now that best that might be given here would be that you learn to deal with the temple of the spirit, or the body, and understand the purpose of the life even as has been given. And as you would attempt to grow, then attune the self. Not that you would communicate with a personality or one another here in this way, but it might be well, particularly for these two, for the study of history or that nature of each tribe upon this plane; for there is the erroneous teaching among you that the understanding of the Christ or the force of One came only through those methods of Judaism [that were] then passed down to Christianity and spoken in this time. But if you could understand, that message was sown throughout the earth in all ages and all times, and the Huna of Hawaii passed in its purest form the teaching concerning the Christ, the Son of God. So as well it was passed among those of the Red Race in this land and so many of the others.

Now if you would understand that which was their guiding principle, you would understand here what it takes … to be harmonious with the physical body and so cause it to respond. Thy flesh is the indication of the thoughts of thy soul, and if it be unhealthy or not forming well, it is because those processes or thoughts or that dealing with spirit is not going well. There is not a man among you who could be spiritually healthy and physically ill, for the physical manifests that truth of the spiritual. Remember that mind ever is the builder and so comes through spirit, and the physical is only the outer manifestation … if you could understand that your body is only a symbol. Understand it, see it as a symbol.

This would be as the drawing upon the blackboard that the mind, the soul, might see, and is the only reason for the body: that there might be given a point of reference for the soul to look upon and see that this is what I am developing. Then use the body and surround it with those colors of brightness, of happiness; and as you would show forth happiness, brightness, so then you would show forth the presence of God.

Now, how would you grow spiritually? Assume that you are God, that you are the Father, of His nature – and in all you do, in all you speak, in all you express, express thy nature, that nature then being the nature of God. Now if you would grow to be a man in this plane, or [grow], in thinking of the physical, from the child to the Father, then how would you grow and how would you mature as is described on this plane? Would you not imitate those actions of the earthly father or the daddy? Does not every child attempt to imitate that of the parent? Then so, spiritually, would you grow [and] begin to act like God, and so, naturally, [become] not that which would be taken in through the eyes or that you would study – though these are then points of reference that you might understand what God has created in others.

And if you would understand or attempt to emanate, to imitate God, look upon the Christ – He who walked, that one that you have record of and know that He accomplished same. If you would look for an example, then, look at that one who is recorded as an example – or Jesus, the man of Galilee – and imitate that life and the manner in which He taught. For did He not do all that we have described here? Did He not learn the healing in the caves, then, above the Jordan, and did He not manipulate the limbs of the sick, and did He not learn to strain even from those muddy waters the algae that grew there and give for the healing properties? Was He a fool when He sent the man to bathe the eyes in the muddy, the dirty, the seemingly filthy river Jordan? Did He not know those elements and those trace chemicals that were there, even that operated? Was it not wise that He did so? But it was no accident. Then understand that which He accomplished. He used the earth and even the mud, even the spittle in the clay there for the reason that He understood the earth and the properties thereof and was able to apply them.

Then, as you would be able to understand this planet, this ball of clay, so you will understand that this is an expression of God. There is no physical and spiritual; there are no separations. Understand that dichotomy, that duality is only in the mind of man, if you would understand those principles that are the principles of God as opposed to those principles of men.

Now see it thus: Man believes that there is the physical and spiritual, and that the two are different and separated. Man believes that there is time and space, and these become limitations then to man and cause him not to be God, for God is by definition He who cannot and does not respect the limitation of time and space. And for this reason He is in all places at all times, but simultaneously. And in that moment that you begin to realize and expand the consciousness to do the same, in that moment shall you become one with the Father.

Then, begin to understand that all these are but manifestations of the thought of God, and as you think with the Earth, so then shall you apply the Earth in all its purposes and all that it might accomplish.

So then, begin to understand life for that which it is: the manifestation of the thought, the nature, the spirit of God – and be Him. So will you grow spiritually. It is simply a natural process that the child would grow to be the man or the mature adult. So it is the simple and natural process that the spiritual child will grow to the nature of the Father as he realizes His being or that which he would attempt to emanate. Then, as you begin to understand God and the nature of God, and as you begin to see Him, then you will begin to imitate, to emanate Him who is the Father.

Now find Him within yourself, not in the writings of a wise man. And as long as you would consider any man beyond you a wise man, a teacher, so would you limit yourself to recognize that teacher who taught Him. The wise man – even this channel and others who would speak those words or truth – that man who taught, or that being who taught him all that he would know; that Being is in thine own heart, Then, if you would understand the nature of God, then begin to teach your teacher, so you would understand then that you are taking from within the self, from your own very nature – that nature of God, that nature that made the wise man wise. Limit never the self, but understand that thou art God.

5022 (7-25-73)

EXCERPT 51

Conductor: What warnings can you give in relation to television and radio, movies, newspapers, magazines?

We would find that that which would manifest in these manners as communication on your plane would reflect the nature of thinking on this plane; that which has come as disease is often given through these media into these bodies. We preach not doom, but seek that you would be aware that you have given yourself to the control of others in receiving into self without sorting out these things which you would accept, that which you would find as entertainment.

Now if you would understand self, see that diet that you would feed to the subconscious mind; be aware of that which you would watch and that which you would entertain self with and you would see that food that you are assimilating for spiritual growth.

2008-3 (2-23-73)

EXCERPT 52

Now see these things in developing the discipline, for these are the particular pattern of this one. As there is the arising in the morning time, examine the purpose for the day – each day. And give the self, yielding, yielding to His presence, and speak, "This day I will be directed of God Himself, within." And in such a way dedicate each day to His purpose.

And yet in the giving of self and in the knowing that these are best for me, never assume that others would best be trained by those same methods, for that which has worked well in thine own life may not be that which another would need. But better that you develop the patience toward others and understand their lack, that that which is within their soul that would cry out to the Divine has not yet developed the understanding of such a need as you would have in the self.

Or, see in this manner: That here would be one who develops a longing in the heart to express God. Yet he would not know that this longing is toward God, and his form would take the expression of painting, of drawing, or of another sort of way; in the preparing of food, or any of those creative acts. Yet this one would seem to have no need within himself, or not recognize the need for discipline here, or for the developing of the physical; or would pay no attention to that which he would put into the physical body. And this, then, would cause that man, who has been so convicted within his heart, great distress, for he would look upon this one and say, "This one suffers, for he would not care for the temple of the Holy Spirit."

Yet, understand those reasons, for one's mind, his consciousness, has been directed toward a purpose and so he would develop that purpose at that time, even yet tearing down those other things ...

and it would be so. Yet that one who would see that distress and cause distress within has been directed toward the development of the physical body, as is his purpose in this time.

Then, what do we attempt to express? Know that each develops in his own time, in his own way; and as you would see one seeking truth concerning that which you would know, then share with him. But if he does not seek or is not receptive, be patient and condemn not, but know that one day when the need is awakened, then he will attempt, will seek. And pray then that truth will be available, that one will come, that the teacher will be there.

Now know that it is for this cause that there is disease among some – that some have not recognized the need to deal with the physical. Yet understand that if a man will not listen, then so disease may come, or physical handicap; and consider it not as a pity, but the attempt of those masters on inner planes to jolt the consciousness, to stimulate the awareness. For was it not so in thee? Was there not provided that moment when thy consciousness was stirred to the need for respect to the physical and the development thereof? And would you not be thankful for that which came? Then see this in others.

Then we would attempt to teach in these ways, that never should one attempt to impose that which he has learned – though it be truth – on another, yet gently lead, and with much patience, for this needs to be developed in this time. And love, and condemn not, but only offer that which another would need. As you are attracted thereto, share, and if he would turn aside, then wait, for one day he will come. Ever plant those words of truth. Leave the fruition, the harvest, to God.

8031 (7-23-73)

EXCERPT 53

Conductor: If I have known God, why am I so far away, and how can I now serve Him?

Now consider this. There are many levels of knowing God, for it is spoken and may be found in that book you call Holy. The devils also believe, and tremble. Does this mean then that they are saved, that they are regenerated, reborn in Christ? It means only that they are aware of God in His knowledge, in His power. So the same is true of many men, both those who live today and those of the ancients. You will find in the first chapter of the Epistle written to the Romans by the Apostle Paul that description of the condition of many of those who have been spoken of as possessing the wisdom of the ancients. For even as they knew God, they glorified Him not as God, preferring to elevate themselves as knowledgeable creatures in vanity and pride, showing their wisdom rather than that of God. Read the first chapter of Romans. You will be astounded.

The answer is that realization that self is nothing without God … Owning one's self means no possession at all, except that it is committed to the purposes and the service and the growth of God, for how big is man? Can one man say, "I will serve you if you will give me this gift."? Will you dare bargain with God, but take that which you have already been given? This is all you have to offer as a sacrifice before God.

What then would be meant by being crucified with Christ? It meant simply this: That Christ, seeing the suffering of man – all mankind as a result of sin – took pity on them, and realizing that nothing could be done outside of giving His very life, this then is what He gave, that they might come to God. What would He require of you? The same! What less can you give than your life?

As has been spoken, the Lord is most pleased with His servant, any servant, when that servant brings another and helps him to recognize the glory, the beauty, the love, the indwelling, the new life in Christ. Even so, as this channel introduced you to Christ, you introduce another to Christ, and he goes out to bring another. This is how the word is spread. This is how the kingdom is built. This is how the world, the very world in which you live, is changed and prepared for the coming of Christ. Be not the one, therefore, to break that chain. If this gift is given to you, pass it on to another.

Now for all those who would commit themselves to God, let them read this message: Find in your heart that you would commit yourself totally to God. Then, acknowledging His supreme Lordship, ask sincerely on your knees that He live in your heart and become Lord, absolute ruler of your life, remembering this one thing: you cannot have God until you want Him more than anything else. The day that you build that temple as a fitting temple, as a dwelling of the Holy Spirit of God, much greater blessings shall you seek and find from that Divine Source, for we would not discourage you as you seek to do great things for God.

Why would you seek God to do for you those things you can do for yourself? For, in so doing, you limit those things He could do for you, those greater things that you are helpless to accomplish. When we seek to rely on God to do for us those things that we might have done for ourselves, we put, in a way, a block before those things that are so much greater that God will do. Be not guilty therefore, [but] through the studying together on the scriptures;

through meditation – as might be explained [as] attuning the heart, knowing, realizing, recognizing the indwelling of the Holy Spirit of God – this is meditation; and through prayer – tuning your own will to the will of God, that your every purpose and desire will be only the will of God; then going out to tell others of His power, of the glory, of the joy of Him that dwells in you.

We could say, therefore, in the words that have been given, "Go ye therefore and preach the gospel to every nation, to every individual, all those who live about you." Knowing that you will be guided by that Source on high, that same One who lives in your heart, seek to be a blessing to those about you; and in doing so, you will be blessed.

2402 (3-1-72)

EXCERPT 54

First of all, we would see one who sees himself as constantly striving and constantly failing to meet a goal; one who has had many blessings and felt peaks, as if on the mountain top in a spiritual sense. And he returns again to the plain, wondering why he cannot go on higher and higher and experience those spiritual blessings that would make him feel confident and competent in his heart to do those works that are of God.

Now we would have that one look at himself in this manner: As the physical body is born in the womb of the mother, it grows, and by degrees it achieves that growth whereby it might sustain itself outside this comfortable womb with all its needs provided by the body of the mother.

Now once this growth is attained, there is a struggle that you know as birth. Compare this with what is happening in your own spiritual life. A seed was planted. An awareness came then, but the entity was surrounded in the protective surroundings of God, was given nourishment through those around him that knew of God, and has grown. There is a struggle now to break out of that encompassing womb where might be revealed the things of the spiritual world. You must prepare yourself for this new experience in Christ this time, when you yourself can realize alone a contact with God in your own heart. These struggles are a constant part of spiritual growth.

This one must realize that there will never come a time in this life when he can feel completely confident of having attained that level of spiritual growth which will sustain him from day to day, for we will find that yesterday's victories are not meat to today's needs. Victories over sin and flesh and the world must come daily in the life. That which we attained yesterday is a stepping-stone to that level we will attain tomorrow.

But remember that one can also slide back, as well as going forward, by not seeking today those things we sought yesterday as another stepping-stone for growth. If you attain that level you seek, that level that you fancy in your mind, would you not then become static on one level of service to God? Would you even want it that way? For we find that even once a soul leaves this plane, this earthly plane on which you live, there are still more stages and higher stages of growth to be attained. Would you seek to attain all that in this one short life? Then remember that as has been given: "Seek ye first the Kingdom of God. All these other things shall be added unto you." Seek ye daily the Kingdom of God.

2407 (3-22-73)

EXCERPT 55

"Father, would you make these temptations lighter for me? Will you take these temptations away from me, so that I'll be sure that I won't stray from you?" For this is the question really in thy heart. But understand this lesson, and then see if you could ask the same question. Thou art made strong by exercising the muscle of prayer and of the spirit. If God took away all temptation from you as a Christian, would you ever become strong? Would you ever become a man of God? There is put before you those opportunities to sin, so that in God's name you may reject these opportunities for sin, and instead choose opportunities for service to God, that you might be made strong.

Now I have a message for you to carry. I have a mission for you to perform. Would I send one made weak by lack of exercising the will, the power of the Spirit of God, the power of prayer? No! I would not take those situations of temptation from thee, but there would be in thy path every opportunity to sin. There will be that evil one, that one called Satan, that will tempt thine heart, that would try you as by fire.

Now the ball is thrown back to thy lap. Wilt thou be strong for God? Wilt thou be made strong enough to perform the mission that I have set aside for you? Ask not that God take away temptation. Ask rather that you be able to meet that temptation with strength, and turn it into a victory for God.

2413 (4-9-72)

EXCERPT 56

Your greatest work is in your own personal life and development. Would this then be selfish? Indeed it is exactly opposite that, for this reason: That which must be done in your own right is the casting out of self – forgetting of self – for in so doing, you become one who belongs to all, for all are a part of God and as you belong to God, you belong to your fellowman. And in becoming this on this earth, you become as Christ, preparing the way for Christ. People will see God and His works manifest in you and in your life.

Now as to those you would inquire about, that you may witness to those dear to your own heart, that may be brought in and become a part of your group and share these glorious blessings, we would give this: Make known to them the joy of God. That as it has come to you, as they see God manifest in your life, even so may they accept it. Testify as to what has happened to you with faith in God in your heart, and these will come in great blessing to serve with you as part of this work.

Now see these things and ponder them in your heart that you may grow. And realize this: that those things which come now to you through this channel – it is the will of God that, rather than through this channel, that He may speak to each of you personally in your own heart. Would He then have each of you become a channel, the way as this one through which we now speak? Understand this – that this is not so – because it is not necessary. And as it becomes unnecessary that this channel be used in this manner, this will cease to exist – even through this channel. For what reason does it exist now? Simply that there might be a voice among you who can express outwardly what comes of God in each and every individual heart. And we would have you understand that nothing has come to the mind or the heart of this channel, nothing has been spoken through this channel that you each may not feel, see, hear, realize, and speak of through that same God who lives in your own heart.

You ask then what of the Initiates? Must one be an Initiate to experience these things of God? We would answer it no. This is not the criterion as has been given. It is simply that those who were, those who had these experiences, had as might be called a head start before each of you, because they had knowledge of God from ages past. And it was with more ease that they approached; and it was with more ease that the knowledge of God was spoken through these, that it might become known to each of you. Seek then those things of God in your own heart. The knowledge of God that has come through this channel to you, in the language which you now speak, all this knowledge will be poured out in your own heart and your mind, will become real to you, in a way that far surpasses anything that can be spoken through your language, because what will come to you will be a sharing of the experience itself. Rather than hearing of God, rather than learning of Him through words of another, you will experience God. You have had an inkling of that tonight, and before, in your own individual experiences. Could that be expressed? Could that blessing be told, that another might understand? You realize that it cannot. There are limitations of language. God is not so limited. Therefore, we find that when this channel is shut off, when no longer are these readings given, that what will be given in its place will be far greater. And it will dawn inside each of you as the words speak directly from God, going through no channel, but God expressing Himself in all knowledge, through the heart of each one of you.

Now this then is that great blessing that God has in store, that each of you may realize; as has been given before, the great arms of God are weighed down with the enormity of blessings from His storehouse waiting for each of you. And impatiently He waits, that they might be imparted. Grow now, little children, into men of God. Prepare your world for the dawning of the day of our Lord.

This then we would give. Know that all you may tell another of the Master is what you have experienced of Him. How can you tell another what Christ will do for him, and in his heart, and in his life, until Christ has done that for you? In what other way may you demonstrate to him the power, the abilities of God, other than what has been done with your own heart and life? Have you no victory in God? Can you offer another a victory that you do not have? This then is the beginning of witnessing, that others may know. The beginning of witnessing is building that life, that they may see. If one should inquire why thy life is pure, would it not then be easier to tell him? Would you then be so much like Christ, that men may notice and glorify the Father which is in Heaven? You will not need to seek opportunities to witness when the life that you live witnesses in itself. Then those things you know of Christ, from your own experience, will be sufficient to tell. The enriching of your own heart, recalling to remembrance in your own heart, will come then from experiencing His scriptures. Make them a part of your life.

Now in your studies, as you seek to correspond those things of scripture, those things of God – with scientific advances – you begin to doubt those things of God when they seem not to correspond with the theories, the teachings, the laws of the scientists. May I offer this bit of humor and wisdom that you may think on it. Would you study music under a tone-deaf psychiatrist whose wife ran away with the organ player??? Seek those things of God, from God; and your heart will be blessed.

Remember the words of the Apostle Paul, "I am crucified with

Christ, but I die daily." Entering then into your own moment of quiet meditation, you must die daily to the world, and the things of the world; and give yourself daily anew and afresh to God that He may work in your life. You seek then a blessing that you may know that you have accomplished something for God. My little one, this I would give to you for this blessing. Know that the greatest that you have done in your short life in Christ is that loving deed you did for another in the cleaning, the menial tasks that you performed in love. Is it then because this was done for one who is a special one of God, or for one who is a teacher, or for one who means something special before God? This, of course, is not so. The reason for the blessing, the reason for the spiritual growth, growing from a task of actual physical labor is the spirit in which it was done; the reason for which it was done. For we find that even in washing dishes, it was a task done that one might please his Master. It was done then for God, and not for another of the physical plane. The lesson here to be learned is the lesson that Christ taught: "In as much as you have done it for one of the least of these, my brethren, you have done it for Me." God smiles and gives His thanks, even for little works of this type. Would you then rather have preached before a magnificent congregation? You would not have done more in the sight of God. Be blessed then by doing those little things of love, daily, for others around you; and know that God is pleased.

2409 (3-29-72)

EXCERPT 57

Conductor: Are instruction or spiritual lessons given during dream states?

Very often, yet there are many purposes within the dreams, [such as] for the analysis of self or the evaluating of self, and that of facing the laws of karma, or constant re-evaluation, or the grading or the testing as might be considered, or the giving of grades for those performances in these planes. Now these [are] given within the self primarily, and with that coaching or the understanding, the teaching of those masters on inner planes, there is as well the writing upon the Akashic record or the recording of that as has been the experience of a consciousness during that period of the day. Much occurs during these periods of giving the self to the rest, to the recupera-tion – this being only a minor part of the portion of the night. But seek to travel, seek to develop. Make those times, those periods of the night of much use as you would seek to communicate with the Maker, with the Father. So, He would manifest, and so periods of spiritual teaching will come.

4030 (7-24-73)

EXCERPT 58

There is the questioning here concerning those classes, those visitations of the nighttime, and those periods of the dreams.

We would find indeed, this one has often been accompanied to those classrooms, as might be expressed, or those planes, those levels of existence in which the mind, as you call it, becomes as a sponge or becomes as that recording instrument that receives knowledge. That which has been referred to as innate is added here so often from the experience of others, from the experience of self and from those who care – who would communicate during these periods of rest and relaxation.

Now if there would be the memory then, the developing of the ability to remember these periods of the nighttime and these periods of the dreams, we would give these instructions. In three ways would these be developed:

First of all, by taking the notes during the nighttime, waking each time after those periods of travel, after those periods of dreams. Then set aside, for the self, the pad and the pen and the light that can be used spontaneously during the night. As there is the awaking, give importance to those feelings, those impressions, those mental pictures that come. Expect these and record them immediately, giving the interpretation then, the following day.

Now in giving importance to these visions – these dreams of the night – these instructions – so will they grow as this becomes habit. Then wake the self often, following the dreams, following the night visions that there will be given the importance. These will begin subtly, and there will not be the ability, often, to interpret that which comes. This ability, however, will come with the greater familiarity with that one who comes to carry you away to these other places, those abodes of the Father.

[Secondly], further develop, by those periods during the day when there would be the stopping for the meditation, and the giving of self to the travels on those inner planes, Now in these periods you will let the mind float free, establishing only, within the self and to the Father, that prayer stating the purpose for so coming, "That my purpose is spiritual growth, that I come now for instruction, not only that I may float freely at this moment to inner planes, but as well that I might be given interpretation of that which has come in the night."

Then thirdly, in preparation for the nighttime, there will be the period of meditation before the sleeping. And in going softly to these inner planes – these quiet places within – to the temple within the self, there will be the affirmation here: "This night I offer myself to be taken to those realms in which there is the teaching – the preparation of the soul for the release of the confines of this human body – where I may be prepared within myself to be released from these low rates – these slow rates of vibration – that as the transmutation comes, I may be lifted away from this earth, away from this self, and that during this period of the night I may be building that light body – that body of light in which I will be able to travel with the Master as He comes to call me then to these higher levels of consciousness."

Then these three steps will cause the ability to remember those travels of the night period, and to understand those dreams, those visions. First of all, the recording of these, faithfully, as a habit. Secondly, the meditation during the morning time and accepting the interpretation, giving greater understanding of these. And third, the period in the evening of preparation of self and the asking, the seeking for those periods, for those instructions.

So as these are done faithfully, we would see this seeker who comes, transmuted into a creature that hardly will be recognized by those about her. For that light, this is so often now held within, will beam forth – will shine forth, and the radiation from this body, from his force field, will be so great that those about will be aware of the change, of the growth.

Now this will take some time. This will take a period of about ninety days. But know that those periods will be noticed.

Now free the self often to the promise about. Drink often deeply of the breath of Spirit that surrounds the self. And feel that light which radiates – which emanates from the self. And know that thou art equally responsible during those periods of the working hours for giving forth His presence – [even] as during those periods that you would meet with those with common interest – sharing of the Spirit. Or we might better say in this manner: that even if thou would not speak of Him, the Christ, the Christ force, even if you would not teach and tell of the interests in these developments, [during] the job and in the daily activities, others yet will know and will grow and will be drawn closer and will see the inner strength and the confidence. As these are built within the self, there will not need to be the spoken word. Then others will come for advice, for learning, for counsel.

And would it not be [right] that it should be so? For how would one develop and grow to be so close with the Father without His presence emanating even from the features, from the countenance?

Be more aware of Him, not only within the self but be aware of His vibration – His radiation – shining forth from the self. And know your responsibility for raising the vibrations of all who are about.

1015 (4-11-73)

EXCERPT 59

It should be given that the development of discipline, that is consistent growth, is more important than direction of growth. It would be better that a thing not be begun at all than to begin and leave it off. Now set the sights within the self. If there would be the direction and growth, if there would be the undertaking for spiritual purposes, see that it is understood within self and that the direction comes from within. Having come then, having set the course, set your sights upon a goal and pursue it. See that development is steady and consistent. Follow the discipline that would be given within, particularly in the understanding of the dreams, for these often will be visited during the night hours by those who have been the brothers on other planes and seek to help, to assist in the work that is being undertaken in this plane, in this day.

Understand then, that there will be the messengers even from the throne that will come for instruction in the time of the dreams, the night visions, for the direction of this work. And often when there are questions asked during the day, they will come as sudden understandings or dawning of insight in the early evening hours or in the early morning hours following that which was given during the hours of sleep, but was not the realization. See these then as directions from the throne and as fulfilling of the purpose of this incarnation.

Seek often to turn self back in memory and realize that which was developed in past incarnations for there is much understanding, there is much knowledge that need be put to work in this lifetime. There is a great deal of service that has been prepared for thee. There is much to be accomplished in this lifetime. Now set about the Father's business.

144	EXCERPTS FROM THE PAUL SOLOMON TAPES
Conductor: What about nightmares?

There has been the questioning, then, what of my dreams: How may I accept them, How may I interpret them ... which come as fears and warnings. There are often the nightmares for this one, the disturbing dreams, and there would be the wondering [as to] how these may be interpreted. We would see it in this manner: That those dreams that come forcefully enough that we remember them and wonder about their interpretations the following morning are always the instructive dreams. That is, it would be the positive answer here that yes, there is a purpose for the dreams coming.

Conductor: How may I understand my dreams?

Now for the interpretation of the dreams, there need not be the turning outside of self, but we would give these two instructions: First of all, that you would record daily the dreams. You would pick from the dreams the consistent personalities. That is, each female in the dream would be set apart and there would be the comparison of personalities ... which appeared. And see that the predominant figure in the dream, whether male or female, is self. In so doing, in the comparing of the dreams and the symbologies and images in the dream, it will be found that there is a running thread of symbology: that which relates to self. Then one's own symbology must be established in this manner so that self can interpret the dreams. No one else can interpret dreams for you – unless there be the psychic or the intuitional interpretation – but from the symbols they cannot be in-terpreted by another, for the symbols are those established within self. See this in this manner, that you would establish your own symbology and use these.

Now as the dreams are interpreted realize this – that the symbology will change. As dreams are lifted to a higher level, as there is the spiritual progress, the nature of dreams will change, the symbology of the dreams will change. Understand this and expect it, but continue to establish the symbology of the dreams. Realize as well this: that that force that lies inside, that is able to give instruction – that is, the force that is able to construct these dreams and give them for the instruction – is able as well to interpret these dreams. If there would be found the inability to understand that which is being said through the dreams, remember two things: First of all, that person who cannot interpret his own symbology, that person who does not listen to self and cannot interpret his dreams, is the person out of tune with self. See this person in this manner: That the reason there is not a proper interpretation of the dream is that outer self is refusing to listen to the message of inner self. Then tell the inner self, speak to the self and say in this manner: "I am willing to accept what the 'I Am' speaks to me. I am willing to understand and respect you as the God force within me. I know that you are me, I know that you are God, I know that you are giving instructions. I am willing to accept." In this manner there will be the closer relationship between the inner level and the outer levels of self. The self will become a more integrated person and will realize that instruction comes from within.

This one will realize that this is not an entity apart from God, set apart [where] there is no law, there is no sense between the expression of the universal creative forces and that creative force itself. You are an expression of God; see not self as a separate entity separated from God. Become a part of Him, an extension of Him, an expression of Him in His world and accept Him in this manner. See no one else on this plane as being closer or more spiritual, closer to the God force than self. For how can one become closer than you to the God force that lies within you? No one is closer to the Spirit of God than self. You need not turn to others for interpretation, or expression of Him. Get to know Him that is the You of you.

You will understand yourself and God better in this manner, and there will be the understanding of all that religion is, and there will be the transcending, the superseding of religion for that which is true Spirit, God force Himself. In so doing there will be the ability to help others; that is, there will be a light that would shine into the world. Now this is an automatic function. It is not meant that this one would attempt to spread abroad the light of God [for] He will automatically occur. [And] when there is that spark fanned into flame, self will become transparent. That is, the bulb that is not lit is obvious. You see the bulb. Once it is lit, once it is tuned into the power, once the light force shines from within it, there is no longer seen the bulb, but only that light that is shed abroad. As there is the attuning of self to the light forces inside for this one, there will automatically be the shedding of the light of God.

7003 (1-10-73)

EXCERPT 60

Conductor: What is the disposition of my higher self at times of deep sleep?

Not so much the higher self here, but rather that consciousness, or that of the false personality, of the false self, the lower self, that would be disposed or taken to other places here you see. Now when there is the period of entering sleep, in communication with the self or with God, there is the joining here of the lower with the higher self and these are those you find among you when there are the dreams of attending classes here, you see, or going to this or that of the other place. This symbolic then of the lower self joining that of the higher self and being taught thereby you see. Not so much a class here, but rather symbolized as class within the dream state or within the thinking in saying here that I have joined those others who communicate with the highest that is within the self.

Now there is not a single disposition then of the lower self, or the conscious self, during those periods of sleep, yet those many things can occur. For there are the periods of travel about your own plane. There are [also] the periods of burial within the self, you see, or closing self, shutting self off from that which may be learned – this bad or this good – or any progress of these times. There are periods of no progress during those periods of sleep; and there are those periods when the soul is released to the Father and used for purposes of learning.

Now if there would be the prayer and the preparation during those periods of night, we would find this soul always traveling to the higher planes or to the higher self that there might be the instruction and there will be the return on the morrow or in those periods of the morning with the feeling of higher purpose and greater direction and not so much the need for asking here. Then pray nightly and dispose of self by sending self to those higher realms or to the presence of the Father that [there] might be the teaching.

1035 (10-15-73)

Spiritual Growth & Teachings

EXCERPT 61

Conductor: Is the Bible as we now have it actually the verbally inspired, faithfully reproduced, and infallible word of God?

Inherent in this question you ask are actually several questions. First of all we would correct your wording in this manner: The word of God is not written upon paper. Consult your own scripture. It is written thus: The Word became flesh and dwelt among us. There then is the inspired, infallible word of God. His name was Christ. That that ye have is the record of Him, of His life, of those things of Him which were from the beginning and those things of His apostles who walked upon this plane.

As to whether it is verbally inspired, faithfully reproduced and infallible, we would answer thus: verbally inspired in the original manuscripts. They are coming to you from not infallible soul entities, [but ones] who knew Christ and knew God and were inspired by them.

Now because they came through these [fallible] channels, there are errors. And because your Bible has been translated and retranslated, and portions lost and portions added, as you would see it materialistically on your plane, (and if you would see your Bible without [also seeing] God) it is fallible. That is, it is sown throughout with mistakes and errors and untruths. However, no man of God, no man in contact with God, no man with God living in his heart, would see the Bible in such a manner.

What then do we say? What are we saying? That what you have, taken alone, is simply a book. It is reproduced by commercial companies for commercial purposes. Can it then be holy, inherently holy in itself? Yet that record that it carries is the record of a Holy

One. It is preserved, protected and brought to you by the Father Himself.

Then when and how does your Bible become verbally inspired and infallible? We would answer thus. The Bible you take in your hands to read immediately becomes verbally inspired and infallible as you open your heart to God and read through His eyes. It is not then the book that you read but He who lives in your heart that is infallible. Now seek knowledge from your Bible in this manner, and in this manner it will be infallible regardless of words written and mis-produced in translations and reprinting and other acts of men. All knowledge is of God.

And think you are not of God? Look to the conscience in its various manifestations of the Holy Spirit. That which the conscience tells you is not wrong. The conscience does not lie. We may refuse to listen to the still small voice of the conscience until we become less and less aware of it and convince ourselves that these things we do are not really wrong, or that they are just small things.

Now understand and believe these things in your heart, and make them a part of your life – that there are no small things before God. Those things that are wrong are wrong. Those things that are wrong keep us from our God. They place a block in the way that we might not see His face, that we might not receive these instructions, that we might not have His strength, and therefore, that we might not carry on His work.

You ask then, does God speak through us? Consider all those things that have been told you before. Does God not live in the heart of this channel? Does God speak then through us? We would say to you, no. Understand this: We speak to you through God. This being understood then, all knowledge is God and this source is of God. This source comes through you, through God to you, and comes blessed of God for your growth.

#2406 (3-21-72)

EXCERPT 62

Know that knowledge not used is like a poison within the system. That man who learns great knowledge and does not put it into use in practical application, or understand and assimilate, grows obese mentally. Understand that as food sustains the physical life, knowledge and wisdom sustain the mental life. As rich foods in the physical body can be fattening and hamper the body and its health, so riches of wisdom can be to the mind. Therefore, exercise the mind with that knowledge you attain. Use that knowledge. Understand it. Assimilate it.

The man who takes vitamins in the form of pills and tonics, and such things as would make his body like a living drugstore, can only build a surplus of vitamins, drugs, that cannot be used, cannot be assimilated, or [the body] will pass them on. Only those vitamins that are assimilated, only those food values that are assimilated by the body, are of value to the body. So it is with knowledge.

You have wondered why you were not given explanations for this, that, and the other thing through this source – information of all those things that men have wondered about over the years, over the centuries, even back to the times of the wisdom of the ancients. And you have wondered why the wisdom of the ancients is not unfolded before you through this source. Can you now understand? Is it reasonable that you are not able to assimilate this knowledge without preparation?

All that may be known of God lies within your own heart. All will be known of God as you have need of it and as you apply that knowledge in daily life. What then do you have need of? You have need of knowing not more about these things of the ancients, not more facts about creation, not more facts such as the color of the Master's hair, or the design of the robe He wore! The knowledge you need pertains to the application of your daily life, in this day and time, for this people who walk the Earth in the present and those who will come.

#2405 (3-19-72)

EXCERPT 63

Then, to another who has come to work with you, we would give these words. There has been confusion in your heart, for you have come from another faith that is different from [that of] those who serve here. Know this then, that one church is not greater than another, for the church as Christ has established is in the heart. The important thing in your work with this group is that you seek a way to work together. Seek the best way that your life and the lives of others around you may be blessed.

If you would experience a great blessing by testifying to the power of God, by being baptized in ... Him, and arising up to walk in newness of life, and placing of your heart and your life in the work of a local church in which the group might work together, then seek this. But seek first spiritual growth and understanding! Understand what baptism is. Understand what the work of the church is. Understand what their beliefs are and understand what Christ taught.

There is much you must need to learn. There is much that might be sought through the heart in prayer. Now seek these victories in your personal life and know this one thing. Listen to this! Ponder it in your heart and remember it. Prayer is not a group of words. Prayer is not a form. Those prayers that are heard and blessed of God are very often those prayers that are never spoken. Prayer is the cry of a heart in need. Use then this definition when you speak of prayer: The cry of the heart in need, seeking for God. Learn these things, and you will be blessed.

How then will you grow spiritually? Learn those things of your scripture. Discuss them together among you that you may understand. Pray not daily, not weekly, but constantly in your heart, attuning the heart constantly to God. Have those moments of meditation, that God may instruct through the heart.

#2409 (3-29-72)

EXCERPT 64

If you would look in your Bible, in the Old Testament, to that book called Job, and know this: that Job was a hypothetical situation. He was an illustration, a parable, that was given of God, that should be compared to yourself and all the sons of God. And understand what happened to this man Job, for God expressed in His heart, as it were, "This man Job is Mine, My servant. He will be faithful unto Me."

Now repeat that, inserting your own name, instead of Job, for this is the way that God would have you understand the passage. As the Father speaks, "My son is my servant and will not turn away from Me, will not allow himself to be led astray," He speaks your name. "And the son, these [servants] are Mine. You can't lead them astray."

Then that one you call Satan answered to the Lord and said, "You're not being fair with me for you built a fence around them that I can't get to them to tempt them as I would. Now if you would just let down that fence a little bit, that I might get through and present the temptation before them, that you wouldn't hand feed them all these things as you're doing. Then I could get to them with temptation, and they would be led astray. So they don't really love you."

And God answered and said unto Satan, "Do what you will with these, for I have given them strength. They are now men of God. Place your temptation before them and see if they will be led astray. I will allow only one thing: that you will not be allowed to pluck them out of my hand. They may be tempted as men of God."

See yourself in this situation then. And find further the words of Jehovah, God the Father, in the book of Isaiah. And may this bless your heart as it is meant: "Will God then allow Satan to tempt you, to take you in such a way, snatched from the hand of God?" Hear His words: "Will a mother leave her suckling child?" See further in this same passage of scripture and hear the voice of the Father as He would say, "My son, I have your name engraved in the palm of My hand that I cannot forget, that that evil one cannot snatch you out of My hand." Dost thou not believe? Turn in thy holy scripture and see that these words are written.

Then in the book of Job, the Master even spoke of that, saying in these words, "You are Mine and no man shall be able to pluck you out of My hand. My hand is in the Father's hand. You are in My hand. There is double protection. That which I have given the Father, no man is able to pluck out of His hand."

Now one greater blessing, and this should make your cup overflow. How was your name engraved in the hand of God? There was placed on the palm of the hand of the one called Christ, a spike, and your name was driven into His palm, leaving thy name forever engraved in the hand of God. No man, no power, is able to take that which belongs to God.

#2412 (4-9-72)

EXCERPT 65

Conductor: Is there a Hell? Is it a physical place where fire or punishment is administered?

Now as to its physical [existence], consider those that are said of scripture, or those written by the masters, in this way. There has been said and it is written that physical, or that of the flesh, shall not see God, nor will the corruptible see incorruption. Then if that flesh would not appear before God, or that dimension of the Father, or that that is God or of the Spirit is not physical, then how would that of the Hell, or the opposite, or that of the burning, be physical in nature? These are thought of and described as physical for the reason that those in this plane, or this dimension, relate best to that described in such manner.

And what other point of reference would you have then for the understanding? Yet [it is] physical in this sense: that that which is not of God, but rather that built or programmed or of material of the flesh – that which would not return to the Father – would need that manner of disposal or that manner of transmutation, or of change. And this we find as like a fire that would consume that which you would not seek to carry with thee.

Then that burned in the fire of Hell would not be of any use to any soul, any individual, and it is not that reality of the self or the soul, but that of false creation, or of the personality, or that you would seek to eliminate. And give thanks to the Father that such exists or that there is a Hell, that that which I have done that is not of the Father might be burned, as that purified from gold that the dross would be removed, that that which I am would be preserved in its purity that I might see the Father.

Then these exist for the reason of making possible that I would come in purity before the Father.

EXCERPT 66

Conductor: You have before you the Fellowship of the Inner Light. These members come seeking your guidance.

Yes, we have this Fellowship and its members. Now we would not take those questions as have been prepared this night, for here is a message from one that has been prepared and must be given before those of this Fellowship this night. Now we would seek that the hearts would be attuned, that you might prepare yourself for that awesome presence that would speak....

Now I am Halaliel, Archangel of Mercy and Guardian of the Path, and I am come for a warning to this group, that you might be aware of the job that has been placed upon your shoulders, and might take it in the manner in which it was given. For we would have you see that which occurs about you, even on this plane, and that which comes as indications within the heart of the job that has been prepared for you.

Now there have been the warnings given. There have been the many who have been lifted to this plane, and have seen the awesome sights, and have reported those things that are to come.

Now we have seen, and are aware of, those things that exist in the hearts of these: the jealousies, the feelings of self-importance, the desire to do the job of another, the enmity even against God for what was regarded as the withholding of blessings.

And it has been given: "Unless you place your value on those things of value, those things even of value shall be taken away." And that you might know and recognize value, we give these indications, even at this time, that you might be aware of that path for which you are given responsibility and the narrowness thereof.

Now you have made the word of God a weak instrument. You have made it impotent by declaring there is no hell. You have denied the wrath of God and the possibility of punishment. But we would have you open your eyes in this moment. We would see the black River Styx. We would see its murky depths flowing through the crags and the rocks. And we would see perched at intervals in this black and filthy mess, those urchins, those angels of Hell, those imps, that would laugh and delight at the suffering of those of your race and on your plane. And yet we would see those, even in your day, clamoring with delight and throwing themselves into its murky waters, and carrying even their children into its black and disgusting depths. And we would see only one fence that need be crossed from the birth on your plane to this river. We would have you realize that no one could reach this black and murky river that you might see as Hell, as everlasting punishment. We would have you realize that it cannot be reached without trampling upon that which God put in the way. That which you would have to trample on, to reach eternal punishment, would be a bleeding body on a cross.

Then would you declare that a just God would not create a Hell, if He would put such an awesome figure in the way to protect you from the depths thereof? Would you then deny its existence? But know that there are even now in this moment, below your plane, those souls bound in chains that clamor even in this second for an opportunity to take up that body in which you now reside, feeling of a certainty that they could please their Creator, and raise themselves a little higher, a little closer to the Godhead, if given another opportunity. And yet you take this incarnation so lightly!

Now search your hearts and see your concerns, for your concerns are for material things. They are for the income, for the personal satisfactions and lusts and pleasures. Now we would have you realize in this moment that thou art weighed in balance and found wanting. You speak of balance, you speak of service, you speak of love. How oft would you step from the way and look for opportunity to help a brother? How oft do you trample over the body, or go around, when you see one dying?

Oh that we could lift the scales from your eyes and have you realize those inner planes that try so often to help, and even in this moment are gathered about you in this room urging that you might listen and understand the symbology as has been given. Lift the scales from your eyes. Open them, that you might see and might understand and be aware of their presences, for there are guides, there are teachers, there are angels, that would minister to you.

Has it not been written, even in your scriptures, that He has given the angels charge concerning you, that they might minister to you, lest at any time one of you should slip and bash his foot against a stone? And would they often visit, if there would be the opportunity, if there would be the purity, if there would be the clarity of thinking. But is there not more time spent in condemning another than in searching your own heart?

Now what we see as having been established in this spot as a School of Prophets was given high charge and high purpose. But know that with all that has been given on this spot, it shall be taken away, if those given charge concerning these things have not attuned self solely to the one purpose. And if you would take thought of what you would eat or drink or how you would clothe the body, we would have you realize that it is not him that could destroy this body that you should so concern self with, but him that would destroy all that you might accomplish on this plane in this lifetime, in these purposes.

And how long would you toil and struggle in the planes of the inter-between, and hope for another opportunity and beg for another. See what fell on the shoulders of the Master. And see in the mind's eye how great was that agony [when he came back and found the apostles asleep]. How easy it would have been for Him to lash out and say, "God depart from thee. You don't deserve to come to the Kingdom. You're rejecting everything I stand for." We see though that Christ, bringing love to the error in His heart, lifted His hands and refused the temptation to anger.

Oh children, understand this these words from the lips of the Master Himself. "Now My son, if you could have seen My countenance as I knelt in the garden, all would have seen the sweat of the laborer pour from the brow from the agony I suffered for your sins. But My son, understand that the sweat that fell from My brow was not as the sweat that falls from your brow when tired. For the agony was this great, that I sweated great drops of blood, for you, for thy sin. You ask, 'How can I love one who would reject and laugh at my Lord?' Now my servant, if I can love him, how is it you cannot? I was the one who suffered."

Now my brothers, thou hast heard the words of the Master. And it has been given, "Blessed are they who walk with Him and hear His words." Study those things of love and know how you may love the brethren. For as you see sin in your brother, you see what thou has been thine own self.

Opportunity? There are souls in this room, in this moment, that have wasted lifetime after lifetime, and cried out for the opportunity even to be here this night, and have said, "This is the opportunity that I will use for service; I will not become caught up in the things of earth and the pleasures of life." And yet we see it being so. Is there not one among you who could set his light, and turn his direction on that one goal, and, without turning to the one side or the other, make his way straightway down that path that would be the example to these people?

And we would have it known to this channel that even this night there will be placed the touch of this Angel upon the throat. There will not be the ability to speak in the morning. And this will come as a warning to you. That which is given of God as a holy channel will be kept holy, or the service will be taken away. That which God has set upon this place, no man will destroy. But those opportunities of service may be lifted and may be moved to another place, if the servants are found wanting.

Now when you speak of love know what love is. And when there is an opportunity to lift the spirits of another, turn not thy back, for his blood will be required at thy hands. There has been given sufficient warning. There has been given sufficient instruction.

Now realize that you have been set up for a purpose in this place. You are prophets of God. You are aware of these things that are to come. This is why you exist in this day. And would you be caught up in your petty grievances concerning what you should eat or wear tomorrow when your purpose is to warn the world of these things to come?

You have been given a message. You have been given a service. You have been given a charge to keep. At what do you spend your time? To whom do you owe your allegiance? I say to you if you speak not the words of God, you are of your father, the Devil. "He who is not for me is against me." There is no middle road. You have a charge to keep. This is a sacred trust, and woe be to him from whom it is taken away. It is written in your scriptures: "My Spirit will not always strive with men."

Now be aware that the wrath of God exists, and is a holy anger, and is always tempered with mercy. Know that this place, and this Fellowship, rests in the hollow of His hands and has been surrounded with the holy light. And this is the message of the Lamb that we would deliver to you in this moment: That He has placed in your hands a holy instrument, one that needs always to be attuned to the most divine. The attunement would depend not only upon the heart of this channel, but [on] all those that are given charge with this service. Know that He will lead and guide. And be ye blessed concerning these words, knowing that "Him who He loves, He will chastise."

To those who would continue in this Fellowship, we would see the divine charge. And realize that the weight of responsibility that is placed upon you is, as well, a measure of His love. Had He considered you unworthy, He would not have brought you to this place.

Now come, ye blessed of the Father. Let us be about His business, serving always in love, and with a smile upon the lips. Now attune yourself in this moment that you might hear, for He has surrounded this place with a choir of angels.

To the servant going out from you, we will have him realize that the going is attended by an Angel of this mission. You will seek to establish His presence there. There will oft be the opportunity to teach. And be aware that never will you open your mouth to give counseling and guidance of Him, that you would not be led by His Holy Spirit, [and] given those words that would come from His lips. Seek always that this be so, and you shall be a channel of the Divine.

Even so, come Lord Jesus. We are through for now.

#6002-3 (12-3-72)

EXCERPT 67

Conductor: How can we guard against the reaction of anger when we testify and someone rejects or laughs at us and our Lord?

In answer to that question we would have you open your heart to this source. And as the words come from this source, we would have you see in your mind the scene which we describe.

On that night, those centuries before you were born, in the day when the Master walked the earth, He was taken after dinner with His apostles to a garden called Gethsemane. When He arrived in the garden, He turned to the eleven that were left with Him, one having departed. And He said to the group of them, "Now you wait right here and pray." And He went on a little further with two of the others, Peter and John, and He turned to Peter and said, "Now you wait right here and pray." He walked a little further with John the Beloved, and He said, "You wait right here and pray." And alone He walked those last few steps, threw Himself down, face down in the dust, and cried aloud to God, "Let this cup pass from Me, if there could be another way. But if not, Father,

Thy will be done."

Now in that moment, see this, if you will, on the face of the Master. That burden of carrying all the sin of all the world came down at that moment. It did not wait until He was nailed to the cross. But in the garden, the weight of every sin of everyone who has ever lived

No one you speak to of the words of Christ will be guilty of anything that you have not yourself been guilty of. How then can you be angry with him for rejecting what you yourself rejected?

But realize this, when you lift your voice to speak words of Christ, and people mock and laugh in return, thou hast recourse in thy heart to realize that Christ has made a promise. Do you doubt that promise? For Christ has said to you. "When you speak My name, I will use it. I will not let My word return unto me void."

How can this bring anger? Use your thoughts. Mind is the builder. And realize when someone laughs, you can smile and say "My brother, today you reject, but tomorrow you will accept because my Lord promised me you would."

This then is the overcoming. We are through for now.

#2410 (4-9-72)

EXCERPT 68

[The entity was in] the land known as Israel or Palestine in that time when the Master walked here. Now we find that this one was a sister of one who became an apostle there. [She was] born in Tarsus, yet traveled throughout that country and was in Jerusalem at the time of that Passover when the Master gave His life. And this one was walking outside the city there in that last moment when there was the giving up of the life. And there came the earthquakes, and this one standing upon the grounds ... saw the grounds open and [saw] that the hills began to fall, and those spirits of the dead walked about, surrounding the self with life that could not be understood. Or there was no way to relate or to understand that which occurred.

Now see those laws at work in this manner: For in that moment that there was the giving up of the ghost in this One, the Master, so the earth reacted or convulsed, erupted. And not only in that day but even in this would you find it true that, in such eruptions of the earth, there is the shaking within the physical body.

Now has it not been given that [that] occurring on this plane on this planet would occur as well in that more minute, or that copy, that expression of the Earth, the physical body? So as the earth opened up to give forth her dead, so did the eye of this one, or that described as the third eye or the pineal here, ... open. So were those about the earth in that stage of inter-between or the other life ... appearing as spirits. Had there not been the knowledge that this one has passed yet I recognize him here appearing as if in life? Now did it not happen to so many?

Now compare in this time and understand that this is not unnatural phenomena that came because of the death of the Master, except for the earthquakes or the eruption itself, but [phenomena] that would occur even in this time. Now examine that which has occurred in the south of this country or in South America in that time so recently in the earthquakes there, that there were so many whose eyes were opened and saw the dead walking about. And see that which occurs, for so many are taking their own lives in this time for lack of ability to deal with that which they see or find before them, for lack of ability to understand or cope with the seeing or feeling of the dead walking about. For there is not the ability then to come back to the earth plane, for there has been the eye opened, and these found themselves on the plane of the inter-between.

Now understand the reason then that ... [this information] has been given, and [why] so much secretiveness has ... come from these records, from the mediums; that [has] ... come from those people who have attempted to explain for the spiritual development, and [why] so much caution has been taken ... in those [teachings] of the gurus, the masters, [of] those given for purposes of teaching on this plane that would safeguard you. For understand that which occurs, for in the sudden opening of those chakras of the physical body, there is more than can be received. If this trance channel through which we speak were able to maintain the waking state and see all that he would see in this moment, or be aware of so many who are gathered around as if in life in this moment, that mind would not be able to accept it, hence he is protected by removing the consciousness.

Now if any one of you in this moment were suddenly to open that of the third eye or become aware of all those spirits, the nature of those things that occur about the life that is in the atmosphere about you, you would not be able to cope with the understanding, with the realization of it. So that there would be the violence within, and the confusion, the loss of sanity. It has occurred often in those that you treat here for the insanity, [and these might be cured if] there only were the closing, the shutting down of such sight and returning within the physical body to deal with the physical world of that that you call reality.

Then understand the foolishness of those about you who come so often before these records asking, "How can I develop the chakras? How can I open this third eye and be aware of all that exists about?"

Then see that it be so. And study that of the mystical Kabala and those manners in which it was given. Study that of the wisdom of the ancients through the Hebrew tradition. And see in this manner that as you would begin to study to show the self approved to God, so ye would find that greater or higher interpretation of that called here, or corrupted, as Christianity or the Christian gospel. And see that Man who in such a same manner as you would have now, had developed within Himself, a great honor, a great respect for the wisdom of the Hebrews. And that it might become more real to those of the world about then, He descended, having mastered all such teachings in the physical, or mastered the physical body and all the uses of the laws of the universe, of this plane – having become the master occultist or the highest of the adepts, as might be described.

So then He had that choice of going through the central sun to many other planes and created worlds or earths that would have been His. Yet this one came back in that Hebrew tradition that was the path in which He developed and graced it with His presence, walking every step of that given therein, or the teachings, making this come to life. Then opening that book to the world, not giving those teachings, not sitting those at the feet and saying this and this, using the words and such descriptions, but living, making all these laws come to life and expressing them within Himself. [This was] not then for the purpose of establishing a new religion, a new tradition or destroying that of the Hebrew faith, for such was that honorable among Him. But He took this, opened it, made it possible, made it that vibration that would be the salvation of the earth, and declared there is no other way to the Father.

Now see that respect He had. And understand that it is not [intended] that you would accept a new religion. For did He not say, "I bring no new law, but that of the old I make real, make perfect in the living thereof."

Then understand that one who would accept His life and see the interpretation of it revealed throughout the scriptures, for those pictures of Him who lived as the Christ were lived again and again and again in that life, that description of the masters who became [like Christ]. And see that one named Israel, that one of whom He was the descendant or the supplanter there and see that manner in which he became the Christ. For he did so in that time when he wrestled with the angel there, and saw – with his face against the face of the angel and staring right into those eyes – did he not look into those eyes of himself or [that is], did he now wrestle with that highest within himself? And the highest within himself sought then to return to the Father, yet he held on with the lower self saying, "Grace me, bless me, or transmute me," as might be expressed in this time, that you might better understand. So then did the angel or the highest of himself, or that expression of God within him, or that guiding factor … then [succeed in] transmuting it to another vehicle that was able to walk with God and understand His teachings.

Now would it not ever require the wrestling then within the self and the refusal to let go when the higher self would escape from this physical world and return to the ethereal? Would you not then cling to it and express all that the Father is, thus becoming the Christ?

Now He gives no new gospel but only lived that of the Hebrew tradition or that of the masters. Then understand that he who would understand the Christ and His teachings need not cease calling the self the Jew or one of the Hebrew tradition, a Hebrew of the Hebrews, but only [be] complete within himself, having proved that perfect love that came, [for] in such a way was He the word.

Now if you would understand and develop then spiritually, study all that wisdom of the Hebrews, of the Kabala, and of the Christ. For there is no other master who has given such great interpretation of Hebrew tradition than that one who became the Son of the Hebrews and thus their ruler, their king, their life.

#3030 (8-21-73)

EXCERPT 69

Conductor: Has this one's experience with LSD affected her spiritual growth?

Now we would find for this one [that information] that might be given. There are many indications that are not [a part of] the questioning here, but for this particular spirit we would see in this manner. According to the first question that has been asked, we would give that there is no experience that in and of itself is detrimental or beneficial. It is the use to which these experiences are put that bring the detriment or the benefit in the spiritual growth.

Now we would see that which has occurred as being a dangerous process. For this one will understand that there is this force of life that is formed at the base of the spine and is a force like fire that is useful [if] used properly, and dangerous if not handled with knowledge and in a proper manner.

Now there would be the part understanding in this one of those forces called chakras that are the indications of the stop gap, the controls, upon which depends the operation of these kundalini forces.

Now we would find that as the opening of these chakras comes naturally, there is allowed at each level a little more and a little more of the light that would come through these centers of the body. These are the life centers. The opening of these is necessary for raising the vibratory rate of the body, that is, the levels of spiritual growth to the higher plane.

Now these are the seven churches, the seven gates, those forces that are spoken of in the Book of Revelation And it would be well for one to study that book, to see the entire book as discourse on the human body and that which occurs within it as the metaphysical vibrations are raised to ever higher levels.

Now understand that these chakras, these life centers must be opened gradually. See metaphorically in this manner that if a person were blind from birth and suddenly opened the eyes, the effusion of light would be too great [and] would shock the system [to the extent] that he might become blind again from the sudden entrance of too much light. It is for this reason that there are controls on the pupils of the eyes, that they would dilate or that they would close and open to allow more or less light to start from the retina, that the body centers, the nerve centers, would not be shocked by the infusion of too much light in a particular situation. Treat the chakras as controls in this manner: that if a chakra is suddenly opened too widely, too completely, there is too much of the light force that surrounds it that is revealed at a time when the body is not prepared to assimilate that which surrounds it.

Now for every soul on your plane we would give this instruction and knowledge, that you might be aware of what is taking place about you: that it would be given even for this channel that if he could open his physical eyes at this moment and be aware of all the senses of the body, the twelve senses of your plane – if all these were opened simultaneously so that you were aware of all the life forms, all of the manifestations of life and spirit, all the entities that hover about even at this moment, at this second in time, the mind would not be able to bear it. And this one would lose control of his senses.

Now so it would be with this one who has come as the seeker at this moment. Now as there is a tiny opening of a chakra, and as there is a tiny revelation of light coming through a particular level, there is awareness in the individual that something has occurred within the body, within the mind centers, within the spirit centers, that which allows the body to be aware of spiritual truths. There is awareness that these new concepts, these strange concepts have come in and must be sorted, must be understood, must be assimilated into the light. And as there is a tiny pinpoint of light, the individual not being able to understand is likely to feel that the chakra is completely open and that which is being seen through a tiny pinpoint is all that there is to see through this chakra. It is understandable that this would be felt, for until there has been the experience of seeing with Divine Spirit, peripheral vision, there is not the awareness that there is more that lies around this pinpoint. Or, that is, as the chakra opens more and more, that there will be a wider spectrum of the same sight.

Now all this is given in metaphor so that you might understand what has occurred for this particular individual. For as these [awakenings] occur naturally, there is the opening of a chakra. That is, that the kundalini forces, or those life forces, of the basic parts of the body from the regenerative organs and the cells of Leydig would force open the chakra lying at the base of the spine first. That this would be opened only a tiny minute amount that there might be awareness of those things that come as the first awarenesses of the manifestations of light; or, that is, that [through] this creative force in opening, one might be able to understand that all life is a creative force. And until there is the adjustment between the physical body and that which is spirit, these [forces] come as a tremendous sex drive and uncontrollable urge for physical manifestation of that which the body is attempting to spiritualize. If these urges then are carried to spiritual levels there is a tremendous energy toward spirit being produced. If these are expressed on physical levels there is a tremendous physical urge that is produced, and a lack of control in the body. And this may cause a great deal of harm.

If the opening of the chakra then is handled in a spiritual manner, in an intellectual manner, this kundalini force that is coming through the centers of these chakras, that is raising the level of awareness, will proceed to the next higher chakra. And as it is gradually opened, as the force is pushing upon this opening to force it a little more and a little more, as there is a growth, and as it opens naturally, it will proceed to the next higher chakra.

Now all of this is given as background that you might understand that these chakras, these life forces, these danger valves that would prevent these things from happening before they are necessary ... may be chemically opened too much and too fast.

Now in the opening of these artificially, or the forcing open of these chakras artificially or by chemical means or by means of hypnosis or other unnatural means, there may be more light coming in. There may be more awareness even of the good things, for there is not bad in the spiritual realm. There is only the inability to handle that which is good, turning then that which would be good, that which would be constructive and creative ... into a destructive force through lack of ability to understand.

See those indications of the destruction of Atlantis and realize that this is exactly what occurred on a universal plane. The same thing is occurring this day on the individual level. And these people who manifested in Atlantis ... are repeating individually what they produced as a nation from the beginning of time.

Realize this and be warned that these people in this day who are forcing open the chakras with drugs are repeating the mistake of the nation of Atlantis. They are as well reincarnations of the inhabitants of Atlantis. This should say much to all on this plane, that you are aware that this is karma of the Atlantean tribe. Realize that the city [of Atlanta] in which you live has the greatest drug problem in the world today. Realize that [in] your city is the greatest concentration of Atlantean reincarnations in the world today. Realize that you are part of the group karma of this nation and you are watching it unfold. Be aware of these spiritual truths and raise yourself to the level of understanding then on spiritual levels.

Now for this particular one who has had this experience, that chakras have been opened more than the body is able to assimilate and understand, realize all that is being brought in through these periods of meditation and these periods of heightened awareness.

All of these are wonderful and beautiful and spiritual truths. Be aware also that the body is not ready, not capable to receive them. How then will they be handled? Handle them in this manner: Seek not to open self too much. Seek only to be an instrument in the hands of God. And make the prayer ever and always. "Thy will be done."

#2004 (10-25-72)

EXCERPT 70

Conductor: What is marijuana, and is it okay for use in moderation? Also, why does this one smoke it?

We would find that which is referred to as marijuana as the depressant drug inhaled to achieve the calming state or lower the rate of vibration or lower the frequency rate of brain waves, thereby producing a state similar to the meditational state. Now it would be found that these states are well and a calming influence in the body, but the question would be: "Is this the better means of producing this state?" That which is produced naturally within the body is beneficial to the body. That which is forced or produced by a chemical means causes the body, the mind, the creative forces of the body to become lazy and sluggish in their functioning.

If this one would control the mind forces, the spirit forces would develop spiritually. This must be done through the creative forces within the mind, for the creative forces are the expressions of the God force. And that which replaces the creative force of the mind is not well for the body, and is not for the spiritual growth, but only hinders the realization of God consciousness. It would be sought that this one would learn the technique for producing this state or a similar state through natural techniques, that these brain waves would be lowered naturally to the slower or more receptive rates, the alpha rates, or even the lower rates, that there would be the infusion or the realization of the God forces.

Now that which is questioned, of the other disciplines, of spiritual disciplines, will come more easily within this mind when there is produced the natural opening of the chakras, the natural realizations, the natural slowing of the rates of the body, that these may be assimilated and that the God forces may work through, the creative forces may teach from within.

Realize that that force which would seek to manifest and would seek to teach and instruct and make this one more aware, is the I Am force, not affected by drugs. It is not turned on by drugs. It is not brought to the surface by any artificial means. But by the meditation, by the pure form of lowering these body rates, these vibrations, the body is made more receptive to the I Am force, the expression of the God within. Now seek to turn to meditation in these manners, and the marjuana will not be used. It will not be needed.

Now the reason this one is smoking this now is because he has not realized that this may be produced in a natural method. This one has not learned to meditate, other than to use these chemical means to artificially bring these rates of the body to the vibrational forces. Seek to do these things through the natural means. And it will be realized that these aids are not necessary, these artificial instruments are not necessary for the greater awareness.

Now seek ever to tune self to God. Realize that while these forces [marijuana] are not necessarily harmful, they are not beneficial in spiritual growth. We are through for now.

#5004 (10-26-72)

EXCERPT 71

Conductor: What is the most evolutionary thing for all mankind that we should know that hasn't been given in previous readings?

Yes, we have that body and those records and these witnesses and the inquiring minds of those gathered here. And we would see that in the giving of that which you ask worded in such a manner, it would require that we give that which is beyond the ability of the minds to accept. Although that which may be given, and that which would be most evolutionary to the growth of all gathered and concerned here, may be given in this manner, that the minds will be able to understand.

That there is not choice on your plane as to whether or not I would pursue spiritual growth, for these [souls] have been put upon this planet, upon this plane of manifestation, for the purpose of evolving. That which you call spiritual growth is only a portion of that evolvement. Those then on your plane have no choice but to face those situations that are given as lessons for those purposes. Then whether or not one would apply the self for the progress in spiritual growth would be a choice. But whether or not one would face those situations that provide naturally the spiritual growth or are part of the experience on this plane – for it was an attempt to produce the growth or an attempt to return to the Godhead, which thou art, that truest nature, that you came into being on this plane.

Then take care as you face each day, and as you face the situations of the day. For it is not another, it is not thy brother or thy sister, nor yet even that which you would call thy God that you deal with when you make the decision: "I will or I will not apply myself to those lessons of spiritual growth, or I will not give this amount of time or that amount of time for spiritual growth, but I will seek the pleasures of this earth for a time, and I will balance myself in these ways." But know that in that very decision, in the facing of such situation in that manner, [there] was in itself a spiritual lesson. Know as well that that which you fail to face this day, thou wilt face on the morrow.

Now it was given of Him and has oft been repeated, "God is not mocked. Whatsoever a man soweth, that shall he also reap." If you would take the time then that is given – so precious in this existence – and cast it then to the swine, so you will reap. And as you feed the body on that food of the swine, so shall it become. Then in meeting that which has been given on this plane, in facing the situations that you are given to meet in this body, would you then make a choice or strike a balance between the good and the evil, or between the growth periods and that which would be pleasure or that that would be cast away or thrown aside? And would you complain and say, "There is too much required of me. I cannot give my time constantly to spiritual growth." Then see in the choosing of this body, on this plane, thou hast made that choice. Each act, each breath you take is a lesson in spiritual growth. Not that you need growth, but all the time belongs to thy God. Then choose this day whom you will serve, and follow that choice.

That which is most evolutionary that may be given on this night is this realization: You cannot have Christ, His awareness, His consciousness, His body, His light, His teachings, until you want Him more than the world. Self must be crucified. It is not a decision to be made daily, whether I would follow the Christ. But having made the decision, then follow. And use the time wisely upon this plane, that you would build that which would last through eternity.

Know that He has not given a set of rules that you may say this is right, that is wrong, but only that new commandment which He gave that thou shalt love one another. Having said this, then is not all said? For the only sin then is self, and that selfishness that would deprive others of that growth.

For no man alone can grow into the kingdom. It is only in assisting others that you would make your way into His arms.

#3015-2 (5-30-73)

World Prophecy

Conductor: Are we on the threshold of an age of spiritual awakening? Did I return at this time ... at least partly for my own spiritual awakening? Will the experience of the Aquarian age Christ be as an example to us just as the Piscean age Christ was an example? When and where may we expect this event?

Now see in the attempt here to give that we must give quickly, that there have been the many revelations or discourses from these records concerning such. Yet, for this particular consciousness we would attempt to reveal in this way: That you stand indeed on an age, or [on] the brink, the threshold of an opportunity for great spiritual advancement and awakening. Yet, those laws of the universe are such that such a time would provide equal opportunity for the fall.

Now see that opportunity for that you would have. For there can be and indeed should be and lie all possibilities for that greatest spiritual awakening that has occurred since man fell in the garden or lost sight of his consciousness of the true self, or of God.

Now as to the concept of an Aquarian Age Christ or one who would manifest Christ on this level: So there comes that opportunity, yet He who will come and bring illumination to this time will be that return of that same personality, that same consciousness, that individuality who expressed the Piscean Age Christ. Or that is, in the suffering servant of the Piscean Age there was that individuality, that consciousness that was also Melchizedek of the Arian Age. So will that individual return in the Aquarian Age; and see that which is the developing or the raising of the level of mankind itself revealed in this individual who was Adam and is Adam and returns as Adam – Adam being that individuality of the race centered in the one man who was the beginning of the race, or Adam being representative of all that is and in his fall so all fell. In his overcoming, so all overcame. Then the Prince Melchizedek became the suffering servant, so He will return having built His kingdom through suffering in glory.

Know that in the returning in this time He will return in that stately manner as king over all that is and will set up His throne upon this that He has made His footstool through the overcoming or the suffering, of the dealing with all that is necessary to deal with on this plane. And as He would come and overcome and establish His kingdom on this plane, so He would establish it in the hearts of all men. And as He will come and reign, so will all men reign, or those [reign who are] attuned to His purpose, to His consciousness. Understand that … which the Christ overcomes, for this Christ is the Christ of the race, not of the age. So, He would manifest with each age as that which would be the peculiar growth, or the indication of growth coming through that age, so as to complete this and move on into those higher realms, those outer realms of consciousness or new manifestation of all that is and has been expressed a new Heaven and a new Earth as He has prepared.

4030 (7-24-73)

EXCERPT 73

Conductor: Is there anything, such as inventions or discoveries, which we should be aware of that would help in the transformation from the old age to the new?

Now it has been given, and should be observed, in coming before these presences, that as you ask this or that, that you should observe that which comes as knowledge and is given, for it has been given that knowledge that is not put to use becomes as fat or dross upon the brain or the mind. And would we not be giving disservice if we gave that which would not be put to use? Then, if you would ask for inventions or these things that would thrill the mind and would spark the imagination, to what use would you put such information, such knowledge as might be given? But seek ye first the kingdom of God and his righteousness, and all these other things shall be added unto you.

Was the question, then, asked for thrill or entertainment, or that you might be uplifted in this type of thing? But if for spiritual growth, then it may be given that in your lifetime, yea, in the next two years, there shall be discovered those instruments that shall be put to use for the purpose of floating metal or steel or even rock or stone through the air even as now such are floated through the water. This nuclear energy will be used in such a way that it would balance those pressures that would close in about an article, that would equalize that pressure coming from above the earth with that pressure that would push from below the earth, then causing these to sustain themselves above the earth, floating through the air. Then, these would be combined with thrust that would move through the air. In such a way were the pyramids formed; in such a way may such stones, such heavy objects be moved even in this day in this time, and would ... be discovered and announced about the middle of next year.

There are, as well, discoveries in the medical field that are coming to the fore in this time, and [will be] put to use that discovery that would begin the building of nerve tissue, that which man has said is not possible that man could grow or reproduce. Damage to spine or brain tissue does not reproduce or repair, yet it will be found that through the combination of the positive and negative ions within these tissue processes, these may be brought to bear in this time.

3015 (5-30-73)

EXCERPT 74

Conductor: Will I witness the destruction of the planet Earth in my lifetime?

Portions thereof are coming even in this day, and before the end of this year there will be realized the beginning of such changes.

The complete and final destruction of this time, as you see it, would not come within this our time, for there will be other major changes and higher manifestations. There will be evolutionary processes, the changing of the earth as you know it. But this one then, would return to the earth's sphere to witness these differences, [would return] to a new heightened level of mankind – the new subrace as will appear.

For we find before the completion of this time … that even those here on this plane shall see those signs – that even the earth under your feet will seem unstable. And you will see the earth breaking

open as its crust will shift and move. And there will be the noxious gases coming to the surface, and the entire atmosphere will smell of the sulfur fumes. And there will be taken much of the plant life from the plane. As a result, the majority of life as you know it will be taken, will be destroyed, will be changed into other forms.

Those things that have come, as the more horrible predictions, will be realized as coming as the evolutionary process of this sphere. Those who have attuned to this purpose will be given charge by reshaping and reforming and revitalizing this plane. And there will be the few who will be led, as if by hand, to those one or two places on this sphere that will be given as protection and set aside by the priests of God, who are becoming aware of their role in this relationship even in this day. And this mere handful will repopulate this planet from a higher level. This will be the beginning then, of the new root race, the raising of all that is to higher levels of awareness.

We would see those who understand the messages of the stars, even in this day, being able to see that which comes upon you. We will find and it has been predicted that even your larger cities in this time will fall away into the sea, and you have not begun to understand the implications of those times. You have prayed that these wondrous events will occur, and you have not prepared yourself for their occurrence.

Now study the life and realize that you may look forward to the time that even a scrap of bread would buy a bag of gold. You will see children dying in the streets, ... you will see the atmospheres of the planets collide one against the other. You will realize that that which is the mass of earth in this day will take new form and new shape and will be unrecognizable to those who inhabit the earth planes in this day.

Conductor: Will there be any danger for me or loved ones due to the predicted earthquakes here in California and when?

It would be foolish to remain in this area after about two years. There will be opportunities given that will attract this one to other areas at about that time. We find during this graduate study and teaching, that there will be the returning to the Atlanta area because of natural processes; that is, evolutionary experiences within the earth – that is, upheavals, not the changes-and the feeling that it will not produce the danger to this one, but would make necessary the move after a period of about two years.

8002 (12-4-72)

EXCERPT 75

Conductor: Can you give us a better understanding of when and what is to come and what is meant by the coming of the day of our Lord?

As just stated – and this we would explain in this manner as has already come to your attention – you are living in the last age, the last day, and very near to dawning of the day of our Lord. What then will you see? What will be the manifestations of this coming?

We will first see that you are now in the midst of a forty-year period of trial, of testing, for that preparation. And this period of the forty years, which as given through the entity [Edgar] Cayce, was spoken of as being from the year 1958 through the year 1998. These are the periods when there will come those manifestations of natural alterations within the earth's sphere; these things as have been given that: The east and west coasts of the United States will crumble away into the sea; the rising again of Atlantis which is already begun and has already been detected; the changing of the areas of northern Europe as 'in the twinkling of an eye' – and this is upon you; and eventually those shiftings of the poles, which will come in that last time.

Now these are things as will be seen in the earth: the physical manifestations and the preparing of a new subrace, a race of entities lower as you would think than that which is now considered the human race; and then the greatest of all these things which is now in preparation, and which would be then the coming again to the earth of Him who became the Christ. This then in itself is the particular event you are to work toward and prepare for. For no date may be given for this event, the reason being then, that it is in your hands.

Now realize that for this is the importance of your calling. It is in your hands to decide what day that will be. You ask then, how can this be? It is so in this manner. The Second Coming of your Lord, the Christ, will come when those who have been chosen to prepare the way, those who have become righteous in their own life – when they have prepared the way – that the gates may be opened, that

Christ may be accepted, that the Way may be clear, that He may come in glory!

2407 (3-23-73)

EXCERPT 76

There was a period of coexistence, though [we find] Lemuria being much the older, or existing before that time of Atlantis, as would be known.

Now both will be discovered in that you would see as your lifetime, and Atlantis very soon. Those discoveries as have been recently described and as are being explored in this time, would be described as outer islands or outlying lands – not a portion of the continent of Atlantis itself, yet contemporary civilization. And much will be learned from these discoveries and from explorations here. Yet will that capitol or that central city, or Poseida herself, be seen rising in those waters of Bimini within these next two years and will be identified as that temple.

So watch for that pyramid that will rise, for contained therein are the records of the Christ, and written by His own hand [is] that which He intended should be done in the development, or that which He will accomplish even in this age. And there is written upon this tablet His intention for returning even at this time, and [a] date will be given for His manifestation on this plane.

4030 97-24-73)

EXCERPT 77

Conductor: Give indications concerning the future of the Jewish people in this century and in general including the state of Israel and the rebuilding of the city there.

Now if we would look about upon those records of those walking in this day upon this plane, we would not find one of the old souls who has not walked among the children of Israel. So then this takes on the greater meaning of all those who would seek.

Now understand, children, it is not required that one find [God] to be called Israel, [but] only that he seek. Then if you would see within the self that we have acquired this knowledge, or we are the ones who have found truth, and we would condemn those who follow another master, or another discipline; understand that it was the seeking in their heart, a yearning toward God that brought them to such, though it be not seen to you as truth. It is the seeking that will cause these to find. Understand that this is the nation, Israel.

But for those as ... have returned to that land of promise and established themselves there, who come for purposes that the scriptures might be fulfilled, we see exactly that occurring in this time. For these are given as symbols, as signs among you that these would be drawn to the land of their nativity or that land so hallowed, so blessed, by being the cradle or the birthplace, the revealing place, that chakra, that earth center, that navel of this planet, that these have been attracted thereto for this spot that gave birth to the greatest that is among men.

Now these [are] drawn there then, and seem as ones being driven by those spirits within; or those memories of that holy place would bring the selves [to] an attempt to reestablish that that has been the symbol of same, or that holy temple upon the mount here. And we see that driving need within these to establish it.

Now we see yet two more battles, two more wars for this nation. Then there will be the destroying again by earthquake of that place that has been set upon the mount here, and ... immediately following, there will be the attempts then to bring that of the temple of God. So will Solomon's Temple be rebuilt in its own place. Yet this will be taken as direct affront to those other nations for that holy place.

Now [those edifices] of the Moslems will be destroyed in such rebuilding and they will bring that war of wars, and you will see bloodshed as has never occurred on this planet in that time. For this war will surround the earth and there will be found – now understand that just given concerning earthquakes that we have described – that as such eruptions take place on this planet, then there is the removal or the rending of that veil – Did it not so speak? – the rending of that veil between the physical and the spiritual. So then will the Host of the spiritual be entering into that of the battle that will not only be [between] those in the physical body; but there will not be seen the differences between the physical and the spiritual. So has been described that Battle of Armageddon: as these entering from the air or from the spiritual ... taking place in a battle upon this physical earth. So will there be the rending of the veil or no longer the separation between the physical and the spiritual, but all will take new dimension in such.

These come then, and are developing quickly. Observe that speed with which such come, and as there come the times as statements are issued forth from those leaders of that nation saying. "We will build the temple in this spot," look then for the end and watch for His glory, for His light in the clouds. For it exists even now. And see that ball of light speeding here as [an] attempt by those forces of the universe to shed light or bring closer to the light all that is, or give that opportunity.

Now understand, this is God's light that passes so close to this planet in this time, and will shed forth light upon all that are. Now open yourself to that time in that period of the passing the closest of this [Christmas] comet or this ball of light to this earth. Drink into self this light. ... Attempt then to fill the self with the light of the Christ, of God, and communicate with that of His nature and of all who are given to the nature of the Christ. And prepare the self for that end for this light passes as that final attempt to bring illumination. Here it is as if [there] is His light walking through the garden, passing, blessing this planet with a wave of His hand, as the King would pass. See it as such.

3030 (8-21-73)

EXCERPT 78

Conductor: How mill the womens' movement affect this country's growth in the new age, and how am I involved on deeper levels with womens' rights and womens' liberation?

Much of this already has been given. However it should be given that there will be the return of one very much like the one called Judy. Yet that opposite vibration [will exist] or will begin as one who will serve the people and will be coming out of that dark continent [Africa]. She will set herself up as a leader among men, and will subject all men to her rule. And there will come that time that she will declare men to be fugitives, or criminal, or subject to being destroyed. For there will be felt that the planet is populated to ultimate at that time.

Now these times will not last long, but will be for the bringing or the righting of a vibration, or the establishing of an alternate polarity, or the completing of all that must be done that all may be lifted to a higher plane. It is necessary that these [to] come yet are karmic conditions and would be felt as punishment or the return of karma, or the feeling of reaping of what we have sowed for many.

Now that movement as we see in this country, in this land [will] provide these feelings or set these movements in motion, that there is set in motion here a feeling that perhaps we have failed to see this. There is coming that which might be described [as] a sympathy towards this movement that develops ever greater, so that men then begin to lose those defenses against rulership, leadership by the female; and as those defenses are dropped, so the polarity comes closer to being balanced or equal.

Now well that it could be stopped ere that violence, then, swing in the opposite direction. Yet for karmic conditions, because of the many centuries that the pendulum has been in the direction of the positive or the male, so must this pendulum swing to the opposite, to the ultimate, before there can come that balance in polarity, [and] before the planet Adam can shine, can rule. And this we see coming in some ten to twelve years that women should rule, or a woman in particular should rule and yet will set up under herself the rulership of women as such. These things develop with great haste for the end draws nigh and all must be accomplished in this latter day.

1040 (4-13-73)

EXCERPT 79

Conductor: What is the future of the black race?

The important question in this question, is the question behind the question – or why was the question asked? The question then, as we would see it, is, "How must I feel toward my black brother?" We would say it in this manner. In the manner of Christ's teachings on this plane, we would offer you a parable.

There was a Southern farmer, a very wealthy man, who had living on his land, in a shack, a very poor black man. Now this farmer attended church every Sunday, and to outward appearances, was of God. The black man knelt in a glen daily and worshiped God. Now the farmer came across the black man one day as he worshiped, and in seeing him worship when the sun was up and the fields could be worked, he abused him and said "God doesn't look on your kind anyway. Forget your praying. You'll never get to Heaven." Now we would find that there came a pestilence in that land, and both became ill and died. They were called up then to meet their Maker. And as this white man was caught up past the clouds, he caught a glimpse of his black neighbor resting in the arms of a form clothed in white. And the head and the face of the glorious form was wreathed in light. He passed through the clouds, expecting his judgment, when the light cleared and faded; and he looked into the face of a black God. Knowing his own judgment, he walked away – sorrowing.

Now how would you look upon your black neighbor? Look upon him as you would look if you knew God Himself was black! For He is. God lives in the heart of the black man, as He lives in you. As to the future of the black race, as a race, that will depend then upon how you as a white man look upon him, "for as you do it to the least of these, My brethren, you do it unto Me." God seeks out and takes care of His own. The future of the black race and your race is in your hands. As you will treat those, so shall you be treated.

2406 (3-21-72)

EXCERPT 80

Conductor: Our last question is, give information as to the universal significance of the comet, Kohoutek.

We would have you see the significance of the entry of this light in this time in the several different ways and [through] the attempts to draw the analogies or the picture of that ... occurring on this plane in this day. We would have you first see this planet, this earth, as the larger manifestation of the human body and see that of the comet or that light that comes, that fire as might be compared to the kundalini force or the raising of that light through the spine, through the chakras of this earth for the purpose of giving light therein and flooding it with the light of the Christ. Now, understand that comparison may be used in this way: not that we are saying that the earth will be opened in all those chakras in the highest that is within, but rather [that the comet] would affect it in the like manner as it would affect the human body. If that body were ready for that light in the raising thereof, then it would become one with God; if not ready, then the detrimental effect from that same raising of that same energy would come, you see.

Then in the entry of the light, of the fire in this time and the passing of this ball [near] the earth, those consciousnesses, those instruments attuned to the light of the Father, may drink into the self, may absorb that energy of the Divine Creative Force – of the Father, you see – and that consciousness will be raised to a higher, to a new level. It would be as the waving of the Hand of God through the sky and His blessing upon this planet Earth and all those that are as the malignancy within or that out of sorts with the higher growth, with the help of this planet would be as destroyed by the healing hand. Then those manifestations of God would be strengthened by that same hand.

So will you see on the more practical level in this time, as that comet would pass, that that magnetic force or that natural universal force of that comet then will stir and will raise aright the waters of this earth, or will change the tide and will cause those movements upon the shores that will be the disturbances and will destroy cities, will cause a great deal of destruction from the flooding, from the tidal waves as would fall. You will find a rash of suicide among you, of the taking of the lives about this earth from the fear, from the panic, from the inability to cope with that force that will be raised within the system from the confusion in the minds as those energies of the spine of the openings within the self open up.

Now understand it has been given that those things that happen to the larger portion or to the earth happen as well to the microcosm or those lives within the earth; then if those chakras of the earth be stimulated, how much greater will be the stimulation of those centers of your own body? Then prepare them. Cleanse them. If these be ready, if these be prepared, then they will come to that singleness of vision and the eye will be opened and you will see the spirit of those about; or the prophets, those gone before, will be illuminated by that light as it passes and you would speak with them. You will commune with those masters, for they will be closer in that day. They will be far more illumined in that day [so] that you will have opportunity to see in that time those that sojourn on that plane.

Now children, if there be only a handful, only a few among you even, who would attune to His power in that moment and accept that ultimate of that light that would come, you may change that level of existence of all that is in that moment and bring illumination to that planet. If we could find those men so given to God, we will change the nature of this race and will avert those catastrophes that have been predicted and that should come. We will change the nature of the government on this planet and cause these to be further attuned. And these would open as in that time, in those early days when there was the listening to the voice of God, and those governments were set and dependent upon those men listening to God. Those men who become the head, the seat of government were those attuned to the force, to the voice of God in that day. So it will be in this if you give that opportunity so that the voice of God, the nature of God will speak in this time, on this plane.

Now this can be the herald of the returning of the Christ, and has it not been spoken by this force, by this source – has it not been said, "His light even now appears in the sky."? And was it not following,

then, that these looked into the sky and discovered, "Here comes a light from the outermost limits of this universe."? So does the nature, the light of the Christ come toward this place in this day, gracing this planet with His presence. Then know that it is the Christ who passes near as if walking through the garden and would bless this little portion of the garden, as He would pass by.

Now little children then, look upon that light in that time and bow the knee and worship – not the light, not the comet, not that which passes through the sky, but He who is the Light of the World and know it is His light that would light the world and live therein. Let that light that is the light of the Christ live in you and so illumine this earth for His coming.

Now we bless you and we attempt to lift your minds with ours as we go before the Father. Join us. Go with us. As you give yourself in prayers, we part.

8033 (10-23-73)

EXCERPT 81

And there is a message as He has instructed that should be given, for you were there on that day when that instrument was used to pierce His side. And it comes; even in this time, in this day, shall it be revealed and should you understand those spiritual laws governing it, that it should be such, that there was gathered upon His shoulder and about Him, that He absorbed, that He took in, as He described it Himself, all the sin of the world, those vibrations of sinfulness then, were called to come in and surround Him. And in that moment that there was taken the sword and put into His side, His soul was all released. And those vibrations even of hell, as might be described, were given to that sword. And that which committed that most infamous act ever has been given on your plane, became a storehouse for such vibration, such evil and has been passed, even as that Holy Grail was kept by those of the right hand or the servants of the Christ so was that spear kept as a sacred relic by those of the left and used by that infamous one, that leader of Germany, even in the most recent times, so came his power. So then does it still exist in the world today.

As John Peniel will pick up that Grail, so will there be taken up as well, in that land called Italy, one who would be a ruler over this land, one so infamous that those deeds committed, in that time in Germany, will pale by comparison. As he takes up that spear and begins to take the cause of the poor and of the church, so will many be attracted to him and think this is the return of the Christ, and so will he be proclaimed. Know that this comes within these next few days and will begin to appear. Even those who are the students of metaphysics and those who are in those studies of spiritual growth, shall cast themselves at his feet and say. "It has happened, that one has returned, that would unite all and proclaim the law of One." So many will be attracted to him, and he would be called the Anti-Christ.

So will one come, little known, and his works shall not be so dramatic; but he is the Beloved of Christ. Quietly will he gather the faithful, not looking for new converts, not seeking to reveal himself by the miracles, by the crowds; yet will there be comfort in his touch, and a feeling of Christ in his walk, and the look of compassion in his eyes. So will you who have known him and been the faithful be attracted to his camp, to his following. But wait for that day and serve one another until that moment comes when he shall be the conqueror.

For he will destroy the other and set in motion that new system, that new order of all that is to be. It will be his finger, his hand, that will point toward the clouds, as you will see His light, as the skies will open and our Master will appear to make this ball of clay His footstool and set up His kingdom on this earth. Those who have given themselves to Him shall not be forgotten in that kingdom, but shall be lifted above this planet and given those abilities to bless and to speak His name unto all that remain. Those opportunities will come to lift the level of the others, thy brethren, those younger ones who have not yet received. So will you be sent upon the missions and allowed to touch that which has been dross and base and transmuted into pure gold that you may take them as crowns and lay them at the Master's feet. So will His purposes be accomplished in this level, in this time and will you go to higher places, higher worlds, higher times.

Even in that time will it be revealed and will you begin to understand the purpose for all that is, and so will many rejoice as you give of self even as the Christ gave of Himself on this plane. So those opportunities come and what has He said, and what has He given to thee? "Be thou faithful unto the death. I have already with My own hands fashioned for thee a crown of life." Brethren we rejoice in your rejoicing, and that mantle that was the mantle of Elijah, dropped to the shoulders of Elisha, and passed forward even in these times, as some have called the Apostolic succession, we would drop from this place onto the shoulders of the one we have ordained as he would go out bearing the mantle of the prophet. So use all that would come in the heart, and give His blessings through your touch, through your teaching to all that will be attracted to yourself. We are through for now.

1016 (6-24-73)

A Final Word

Now children, know that in this moment He stands near so that you can feel His presence. And if there be one thing that we might express this night that might open up to a greater truth within you all, it would be in this manner: That there is given among you that tendency to understand this or that through the intellectual or finding methods, techniques or purposes; and there is the tendency to reject that which has been seen as piety, or holiness, or the sanctification of the body, or that seen as superstition, as reverence in worship. But understand children, there is a God so holy that you must transcend all that is physical to stand in His presence.

Now begin doing so. Begin respecting this physical body as a temple, as a temple of the Holy Spirit, so sacred, so sanctified that on entering that chapel that you have prepared, you would set aside the world and enter there with such reverence, such holiness, that the character of that place would be changed, the nature of the vibrations would be different, and you [would] enter then into worship without the word being spoken. It would not be a channel, it would not be a minister who would bring His presence, but it would exist within you. There is a God so holy that that body in its natural state cannot stand Its presence. Now It is not only within you, but it sur-rounds all that is in this universe, [and] is alive with the presence of God.

Then open yourself thereto and see how holy that God is. Then make that holiest within you, that Holy of Holies, that He might enter, that you ... might there worship. And in so giving self, in so becoming aware that this God that has been made so natural and a plaything by those who would come about and call themselves the psychics, the spiritual teachers, the advisors here or there, and who would apply those laws and this and that discipline and would attempt to understand intellectually – see that these become humble; and bow the knee and prostrate the self before that most holy God and remove the shoes, for they stand on holy ground.

Now children understand how holy is the Creator, and make it not light or simple among you, but give way to His holiness by dedicating the self, all that is. Respect those bodies. Respect His temple. Respect that place of worship, that chapel that you set aside, and make it a holy place, that all who enter therein would feel that vibration, that holiness, and would begin to worship from the entering in of such presences.

Now so often have these come who are assembled in this moment and bless this place, grace it with their presence and would seek here to abide always, as they have been commanded and [as they] vote to do so. But only their presence is real and felt, known, when you recognize it. And how would you recognize it but make the self sensitive thereto, or open to such presences that you would feel and know and touch and communicate?

Then give self often to that worship in such a manner and make it not light. Make it not a simple exercise. Make it not small through habit but greater each time you come to worship. And less of the earth would be known, less of the physical and more of the spiritual, so that you would transcend this plane, and often you would simply leave this temple behind and walk with Him in the clouds, when He would take the hand and walk with thee. Has He not said that "I will come in and sup with thee, [and] we will eat together of the manna of life"?

He is not so far off, not so far off. He would walk with thee. Open to His presence for He is here.

We bless you as we go in peace.

#3030 (8-21-73)

Made in the USA
Las Vegas, NV
29 April 2023